Huddersfield TROLLEYBUSES

Stephen Lockwood

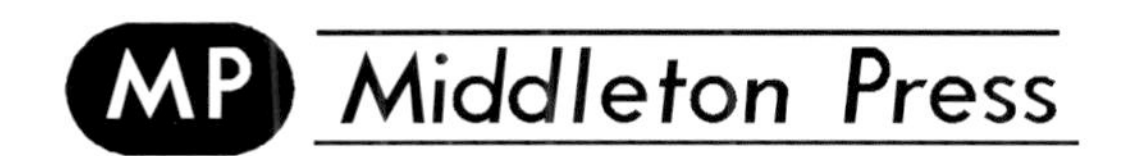

Cover picture: During the trolleybus years, this was the first sight that travellers emerging from Huddersfield railway station would probably see - a spare trolleybus, immaculate in red and cream with poles down, parked in St Georges Square. The scotch under the offside front wheel was normal practice in this hilly town whenever vehicles were left unattended. No 564 was a 1948 Karrier MS2 rebuilt in 1957 with an East Lancs body. It lasted in service until February 1964. (Photobus/J.Copland)

To my wife Eileen, without whose hard work and support this book would not have been possible.

Published October 2002

ISBN 1 901706 92 3

Design David Pede

Published by
Middleton Press
Easebourne Lane
Midhurst, West Sussex
GU29 9AZ
Tel: 01730 813169
Fax: 01730 812601

Printed & bound by Biddles Ltd,
Guildford and Kings Lynn

CONTENTS

INTRODUCTION AND ACKNOWLEDGEMENTS

I spent my formative years up to the age of 23 living in Huddersfield. Our house overlooked the junction of Cobcroft Road and Wasp Nest Road at Fartown on the Birkby trolleybus route turning loop. This is where my interest in trolleybuses began, through watching the vehicles come up from the terminus and make the 90 degree turn. This was a prime spot for dewirements which occasionally happened, though probably not as often as I tend to remember.

In the long hot school holidays my mother, wanting us out from under her feet, would give my older brother and I the money to take a trolley ride to the town - then all the way to Marsden and back, with the possibility of the trolley 'racing' a goods train travelling on the opposite hillside all the way up the Colne Valley.

In 1960 we moved to Richmond Avenue, just off Bradford Road near Fartown Bar and from my back bedroom I could watch the trolleys coming down from Brackenhall, disappearing as they went round the curve to Smithy, then re-appearing on Bradford Road as they came down to the Dewhurst Road stop. It was during this year that I started to travel across town every schoolday by trolley to attend the Grammar School at Almondbury. In 1963, when the Fixby and Almondbury routes were joined, this became a through journey without changing and I well remember the first day of this when new routings and wiring were brought into use. My best mate at school, Trevor Longbottom, lived further up the route at Bradley Bar and always bagged the front off-side seat upstairs for these journeys, and I joined him at Dewhurst Road. A photograph taken during one of these trips is included in this book.

As my interest in the trolleybus system grew, I tried to find out more about their history. Fortunately, at the end of the 1950s, two books about local transport became available One, by Bill Stocks, was titled *Pennine Journey* and was a general historical survey of transport in the area and included sections on the trams and trolleybuses. The other was a detailed history of Huddersfield's trams entitled *The Tramways of Huddersfield* by Roy Brook which described fully the tram to trolleybus conversion. I soon became aware that Roy organised monthly meetings of tram, trolleybus and railway enthusiasts at The Tolson Memorial Museum on Wakefield Road, and for the next ten years or so I hardly missed a meeting. The nucleus of my Huddersfield trolleybus photograph collection was formed by purchases at these meetings from such quality photographers as Jim Copland, Vic Nutton and Roy Brook himself.

What was it that made Huddersfield trolleybuses so fascinating? More obvious reasons might be the hilly routes with scenic views over the town and the use of special braking devices down the steepest gradients. It could be the conservative nature of the vehicles, all six wheelers with two step entrances (apart from trolleybus no. 6) and narrow width, features which were unnecessary in the later years of the system. No Huddersfield trolleybus carried exterior advertising (apart from some small window stickers), nor had traction batteries or heaters for the passengers.

The re-bodying of many of the fleet and alterations made at overhauls (notably the removal of bumpers) created a very varied fleet visually and even the non-standard placement of a registration plate on the cream front dash created a vehicle that could be identified long before the fleet number became visible. Such variety did not mean that the fleet was a rag-bag collection - far from it. Maintenance of vehicles and overhead wiring was to the highest standards and the fleet was generally always very well turned out. A repainted trolleybus, smelling of varnish, was a joy to behold and the sight of one on a test run from Great Northern Street Works is well remembered.

There were also the rituals of trolleybus operation that added to their fascination: the conductor having to jump off the vehicle to pull the trigger for the overhead frogs (points) at route junctions and the palaver whenever a dewirement occurred, which was always a spectacle worth watching.

This work is not meant to be a history of the system, as that has been very adequately covered in Roy Brook's book *The Trolleybuses of Huddersfield* published in 1976. Here, I have attempted to give a flavour of the system to those who never knew it and to bring back memories for those who did.

The photographs are arranged on a geographical basis starting in the north with the Brighouse route, then proceeding route by route in a clockwise direction around the town finishing with a survey of the town centre. The West Vale route is slightly out of sequence to allow the last route section to be Outlane and Lindley as prescribed by history. The photographs have been chosen mainly from my own collection with help from fellow enthusiasts and I am grateful to all who so willingly responded to my request for permission to reproduce their views. There are a few prints credited to a 'collection' whose origin is not known and I hope that these unknown contributors will understand my good intent. The selection of photographs has proved difficult due to the need to keep within the necessary limit of views set by the publisher. I have tried to use, as far as possible, views that have not been published previously, and those which show as many facets of the system and vehicle variations as possible. I apologise if a favourite location or vehicle is not represented here.

My thanks go to the four gentlemen who have read over my text and captions and suggested improvements. These are: Roy Brook, who has additionally kindly allowed me to reproduce maps from his book which were drawn for him by the late Jim Lloyd; John Senior, who early in his passenger transport career was greatly involved in the project of rebuilding the pre-war Karrier E6 vehicles; Peter Cardno, formerly a schoolteacher at Hudderfield New College and who is currently engaged on the preparation of a book on Huddersfield Corporation motorbuses, and Philip Jenkinson, that master observer of the Huddersfield trolleybus scene, whose written account and reminiscences of the system in its last years must surely someday be published.

Thanks are also due to David Smithies and Stanley King for their assistance and to David Ross of Portsmouth for helping me with photographic processing matters.

In conclusion, I wish to pay tribute to all those who worked on the trolleys over the years - drivers, conductors and inspectors, maintenance staff, office staff and managers. Without them this book could not have been possible.

GLOSSARY

Trolley When trolleybuses were introduced ,they were referred to in timetables, publicity and on stop signs as 'Trolley Vehicles' Tickets bore the legend 'Huddersfield Corporation Trackless Trolley Vehicles' During and after the war the term 'Trolleybus' came to be used on these items, although the term 'Trolley Vehicle' did continue in use by the Transport Department on various documents. Huddersfield people, however, always referred to the trolleybuses simply as 'trolleys.'

Petrol Bus This term was commonly used to denote any type of motorbus (whatever type of fuel applied). The more correct 'diesel bus' did not come into common use until the early 1960's, when the trolleys began to be replaced by this 'new' type of vehicle.

Trigger The metal handle on the side of a traction pole at trolleybus route junctions. The trigger was attached by cable to the overhead frogs to allow the conductor to change the frogs by hand as required. The trigger was accompanied by an indication in small white letters of its purpose i.e 'Pull for St George's Square', or less specifically 'Pull for loop'. At automatic frogs a trigger was not always provided, merely a piece of thin rope to be pulled in emergencies when the automatic mechanism failed to function correctly.

Derrick A tower wagon used for overhead line repairs and towing defective trolleybuses, or when trolleybuses needed to be taken to areas away from the overhead wiring.

Rebuilds This term was used by the Transport Department to describe re-bodied vehicles and this is used throughout this book. Whilst the first trolleybuses to be re-bodied had extensively rebuilt chassis, the treatment to post war chassis that were rebodied was not so comprehensive.

GEOGRAPHICAL SETTING

Huddersfield is an industrial town, once famous for its production of fine woollen and worsted cloth, with a population of approximately 130,000. It is situated in West Yorkshire on the edge of the Pennines. Nearby towns are Bradford (11 miles/17km), Leeds (15 miles/24km), Halifax (7 miles/11km) and across the Pennines, Manchester (25 miles/40km). Administratively, since 1974, Huddersfield has been part of the Metropolitan Borough of Kirklees although in the tram and trolleybus eras Huddersfield was a County Borough, having been granted its Charter of Incorporation in 1868.

The Pennines is the source of the Colne and Holme rivers which join near to Folly Hall, close to the town centre. The valley of the river Colne forms a natural passage to the Pennines and is used by trans-Pennine transport routes (road, canal and rail) between Leeds and Manchester. Both canal, and later railway, burrowed under the hills using tunnels at Standedge. The road (A62) takes a higher route here, although its importance waned upon the opening of the M62 motorway over the moors to the north west in the 1970s. The railway came to the town in 1847 when the famous railway station (now a Grade I listed building) was opened.

Huddersfield is surrounded by hills and moorland and this is reflected by a local saying that from every street corner in the town, green fields are visible. The town is dominated by Castle Hill, 900 feet above sea level, and topped by the Victoria Tower, erected in 1898 to celebrate the then Queen's Golden Jubilee. This hilly nature affected the trolleybus routes, the steepest gradients being Woodhouse Hill on the Riddings service (1 in 8.3/12%), Newsome Road on the Newsome route (1 in 9.3/10.75%) and Chapel Hill on the Newsome/Lockwood services, (1 in 10.5/9.5%).

HISTORICAL BACKGROUND

To tell the story of Huddersfield's trolleybuses, reference needs to be made to the tramway system which preceeded it.

Difficulties in finding an operator to run the trams in the hilly terrain in the town led the Corporation to seek powers to run the trams themselves. Thus Huddersfield became the first municipal transport operator when a cross-town service of steam trams commenced between Lockwood Bar and Fartown Bar on 11th January 1883. The gauge chosen was unusual at 4ft 7¾ins/1416mm, the intention being to run a goods service using standard gauge railway wagons running on their flanges in the groove of the tram rail. Although horse trams were operated briefly on a service to Moldgreen between 1885 and 1888, the steam tram network was greatly expanded. By the time that electric trams began to take over from steam in 1901/2, the basic network that was to become the trolleybus system had been formed. The first electric trams were put in service on the Outlane, Lindley and Edgerton routes in early 1901 and within eighteen months the changeover to electric traction was complete. By 1923 extensions had been added to West Vale, Marsden and lastly to Brighouse, where the route included a three-quarter mile stretch of reserved sleeper track tramway between the New Inn, Bradford Road and Fixby. Another innovation was a coal delivery service to local mills using two coal wagons mounted on tramcar trucks. The peak of Huddersfield's tramcar development came in 1931/2 when eight domed-roof fully enclosed luxury trams were delivered from English Electric. These had a short life in the town and were sold to Sunderland in 1938 after the Marsden route was converted to trolleybus operation. They ran in Wearside until 1954, longer than some of the trolleybuses that replaced them in their home town!

Motor buses had also been introduced in 1920, initially operating feeder services to tram routes. In 1929 the Corporation made an agreement with the London, Midland and Scottish Railway Company to jointly operate motorbus services on an equal basis under the control of the Huddersfield Joint Omnibus Committee. Day to day management of motorbuses remained with the Tramways Department (renamed Passenger Transport Department in 1936). Motorbus routes were established well beyond the Borough boundary with most local routes inside the Borough being provided by the wholly Corporation owned trams. In Huddersfield town centre motorbus services were kept on the fringes in Lord Street and Upperhead Row, where a bus station opened in 1948. They were never seen on the town's main shopping streets of New Street, John William Street and Westgate, these being the sole preserve of trams and eventually trolleybuses. It was not until March 1962, when trolleybuses had begun to be replaced by entirely Corporation owned diesel buses that motorbuses came to penetrate these central streets.

By the early 1930s consideration had to be given to extensive renewal of the tramway equipment and, as an experiment, it was decided to convert one route to trolleybus operation. The service chosen was that to Almondbury, and it was also proposed to construct a branch from this route along Longley Road to Lowerhouses. This addition was dropped after opposition from residents, and the Lowerhouses service opened using 'Petrol Buses' running via Dog Kennel Bank. Six trolleybuses were ordered for the Almondbury route, these being combinations of four chassis types and three body types to test the available market. However, all were six wheelers in order to match the seating capacity of the trams. Four of them had Karrier chassis, built locally in the town. Thus Huddersfield's trolleybus era began when Karrier trolleybus number 2, together with Civic representatives, formally opened the trolleybus system on 4th December 1933. The service was given route number 65.

The success of this operation led the Corporation to equip a more extensive route for trolleybuses. From 11th November 1934, 24 Karrier trolleybuses numbered 7 to 30 started work on the Outlane and Lindley to Waterloo cross town service, numbered 71 (Lindley) and 73 (Outlane).

Having proved that the trolleybus was ideal for Huddersfield's severe operating terrain, the Corporation now pressed ahead and obtained powers, under the Hudderfield Corporation (Trolley Vehicle) Act 1936, to replace all the remaining tram services with trolleybuses, starting with routes that still used single track with passing loops. Accordingly, following the delivery in 1935/6 of two experimental vehicles numbered 31 and 32, eight further Karrier trolleybuses (nos. 33 to 40) were ordered to replace trams on the Newsome route. This became service 20 and opened on 2nd May, 1937. The dates of the subsequent opening of routes to trolleybuses from trams can be summarised as follows:

Crosland Moor (60/61)	3rd October 1937
Birkby (81)	7th November 1937
Marsden (40/41)	10th April 1938
Bradley (40/41)	19th June 1938
Sheepridge (10)	19th June 1938
Woodhouse (20)	19th June 1938
Longwood (10)	1st January 1939
Lockwood (50)	12th January 1939
West Vale (30)	28th May 1939
Brighouse (90)	30th June 1940

Some of the routes were extended beyond the former tram termini. The most significant development was at Sheepridge, where the route was extended as a circular service via Woodhouse (service 20) back to Bradford Road at Fartown Bar. Service 20 worked similarly in the opposite direction onto service 10 at Sheepridge. There were other short extensions from Crosland Moor to Crosland Hill, Newsome Church to Newsome South and in Marsden from Peel Street to Fall Lane. The Honley service could not be converted to trolleybuses due to a low bridge at Lockwood Viaduct, and the trolleybus service was therefore terminated at Lockwood. The Brighouse service was re-routed where the trams had a private sleeper track between New Inn, Bradford Road and Fixby. The trolleybuses took a slightly longer road route via Bradley Bar. Coasting brake regulations on steep descents were imposed by the Ministry of Transport on parts of the Newsome, Woodhouse, Crosland Hill, Longwood and West Vale routes, although in 1949 these were abolished on the Longwood section and shortened on others. In order to turn vehicles at termini, much use was made of triangular reversers into side roads and one way loops of wires around side streets. Only two purpose built turning circles were provided, these being at Lockwood and the intermediate turning point at Slaithwaite (Birks Well) on the Marsden Route. Special arrangements, however had to be made at the former Dod Lea tram terminus (always referred to as Longwood by trolleybuses) where the lack of a suitable turning place resulted in a concrete platform including a turntable being built out from the hillside.

Vehicles for all these services were provided by 100 Karrier E6 trolleybuses (nos 41 to 140) with semi-streamlined bodywork to Huddersfield's own specification.

During the conversion from tramway operation, considerable street works were necessary, including the lowering of roadways under railway bridges on the Bradley and Birkby routes. In addition, reconstruction of roads to remove tram tracks resulted in the wiring up of temporary diversions of trolleybus routes. In 1937 the Lindley and Outlane services were diverted via New North Road and Edgerton Grove Road between the Town Centre and Gledholt, and in 1939 the main streets of the town were reconstructed resulting in trolleybus services being diverted via South Parade, Manchester Street and Market Street.

The war years did not slow developments of the system and during this time new turning facilities were provided at Bradley Bar on the Brighouse route and the Griffin Inn on the Crosland Hill route. The appointment of a new general manager resulted in a revised vehicle livery. The two tone red/maroon layout was replaced with all over Post Office red. The cream bands and front 'swoop' were retained and a 'Huddersfield Corporation' legend was placed on the cream band under the lower deck windows. A large fleet number in black numerals was placed at the top of the front dash panel. All fleet numbers were increased by 400 in 1942 so that the fleet became numbered 401 to 540. Apart from the introduction of a fleetname on the side panels instead of the Corporation legend in 1953 and the painting of wheels red instead of black from 1959, there were no other further changes to vehicle livery throughout the life of the system.

On 6th March 1949, long awaited extensions at Sheepridge saw the system penetrating the Brackenhall and Riddings estates. This entailed the breaking of the circular service and abandonment of half a mile of wiring at the Woodhouse Hill end of Ashbrow Road. Brackenhall and Riddings henceforth operated as separate services. The triangular reversers at Almondbury, Crosland Hill and Birchencliffe were replaced by newly constructed turning circles during 1950-51.

The first contraction of the trolleybus system took place on 9th July 1955 when the last trolleybus ran to Brighouse, and from then this service ran only as far as the Borough Boundary at Fixby. The reason given at the time for this was the expense of paying rates on the traction poles outside the Borough. This loss of route mileage was partly compensated for by the opening, on 2nd April 1956, of a short branch from the Bradley service into the Keldregate estate.

At this point it would be useful to list the principal services in operation This pattern of service had been in force since 1949 and would remain in place until routes were converted to diesel buses in the 1960s.

10	Brackenhall - Lockwood
20	Riddings - Newsome South
21	Town Centre - Newsome Church
30	West Vale - Almondbury
33	Town Centre - Almondbury
40	Bradley Keldregate - Marsden
41	Bradley Leeds Road - Slaithwaite
60	Birkby - Crosland Hill
71	Waterloo - Lindley
72	Moldgreen - Marsh
73	Waterloo - Outlane
74	Moldgreen - Salendine Nook
90	Fixby - Longwood
92	Town Centre - Paddock

Some extensions to the system were now in an advanced stage of planning, these being to Balmoral Avenue (a branch off the Crosland Hill route), Dalton (a branch off the Moldgreen loop) and to Deighton, an extension of the Riddings route. However, the tide was now turning against the trolleybus in Britain, and in 1960 the General Manager recommended that the routes outside the Borough Boundary (ie West Vale and Marsden) be converted to diesel bus operation. In addition it was decided to introduce all the above route extensions as diesel bus routes.

Accordingly, an order for Leyland buses was made sufficient to convert the West Vale route on which the last trolleybus ran on 8th November 1961. At this date trolleybuses were still being rebuilt and given new bodies, the last such entering service in 1962, followed by four given secondhand bodies in 1963. Further deliveries of diesel buses resulted in the Marsden service being operated for the last time by trolleybus on 30th January 1963.

The loss of the Marsden service resulted in a major trolleybus route re-organisation including the erection of new wiring in Northumberland Street and Lord Street and the reinstatement of wiring for service use in Northgate. This was to allow the Fixby service to be linked with that to Almondbury, the new through service being numbered 34. The Bradley service was also linked to the Longwood route as service 40, although no new wiring was necessary to allow this.

This period of the early 1960s and indeed up to the end of the trolleybus system was one of great changes to the road system around the town centre. The construction of the inner ring road, involving road widening, dual carriageways, and the provision of three large roundabouts, created problems for the trolleybuses and new wiring layouts and short route diversions were necessary. These works eventually extended on to Wakefield Road, necessitating the widening of Somerset Bridge at Aspley and the remodelling of the junction with the Almondbury service where several temporary changes to the overhead layout became necessary as the works proceeded.

The seemingly inevitable decision to convert all trolleybus services to diesel bus operation was made in October 1962. The remaining routes were converted as follows, with the date shown being the last day of trolleybus operation:

Birkby - Crosland Hill	5th February 1964
Fixby - Almondbury	14th July 1965
Brackenhall - Lockwood	13th July 1966
Riddings - Newsome	13th July 1966
Bradley - Longwood	12th July 1967
Waterloo - Lindley/Outlane	13th July 1968

For the final week of trolleybus operation, BUT 623 was decorated with illuminated lights and operated in normal service. On the last day only a token service of trolleybuses was operated with one vehicle on each of the two services. The crowds in the town centre and all along the route were an indication of just how fond Huddersfield people were of their trolleys. The last passenger carrying trolleybus became 629 as it returned through the town centre and along Manchester Road to Longroyd Bridge Depot at 3.50pm.

R 53474.

IN PARLIAMENT
SESSION 1935-36

Huddersfield Corporation (Trolley Vehicles)

NOTICE IS HEREBY GIVEN that application is intended to be made to Parliament in the Session 1935-36 by the Mayor, Aldermen and Burgesses of the Borough of Huddersfield for an Act under the above name or short title whereby it is proposed to authorise them to provide vehicles to be propelled by mechanical power conveyed by overhead wires and trolleys and to run the same along (amongst others) this street or road, and for that purpose to place and erect posts, poles, cables, wires and any other necessary or convenient apparatus and equipment in and along this street or road.

Dated this 31st day of October, 1935.

SAMUEL PROCTER,
Town Clerk,
HUDDERSFIELD.

SHARPE, PRITCHARD & Co.,
Palace Chambers, Bridge Street,
WESTMINSTER, S.W.1.
Parliamentary Agents.

Alfred Jubb & Son, Ltd., Printers, Huddersfield.

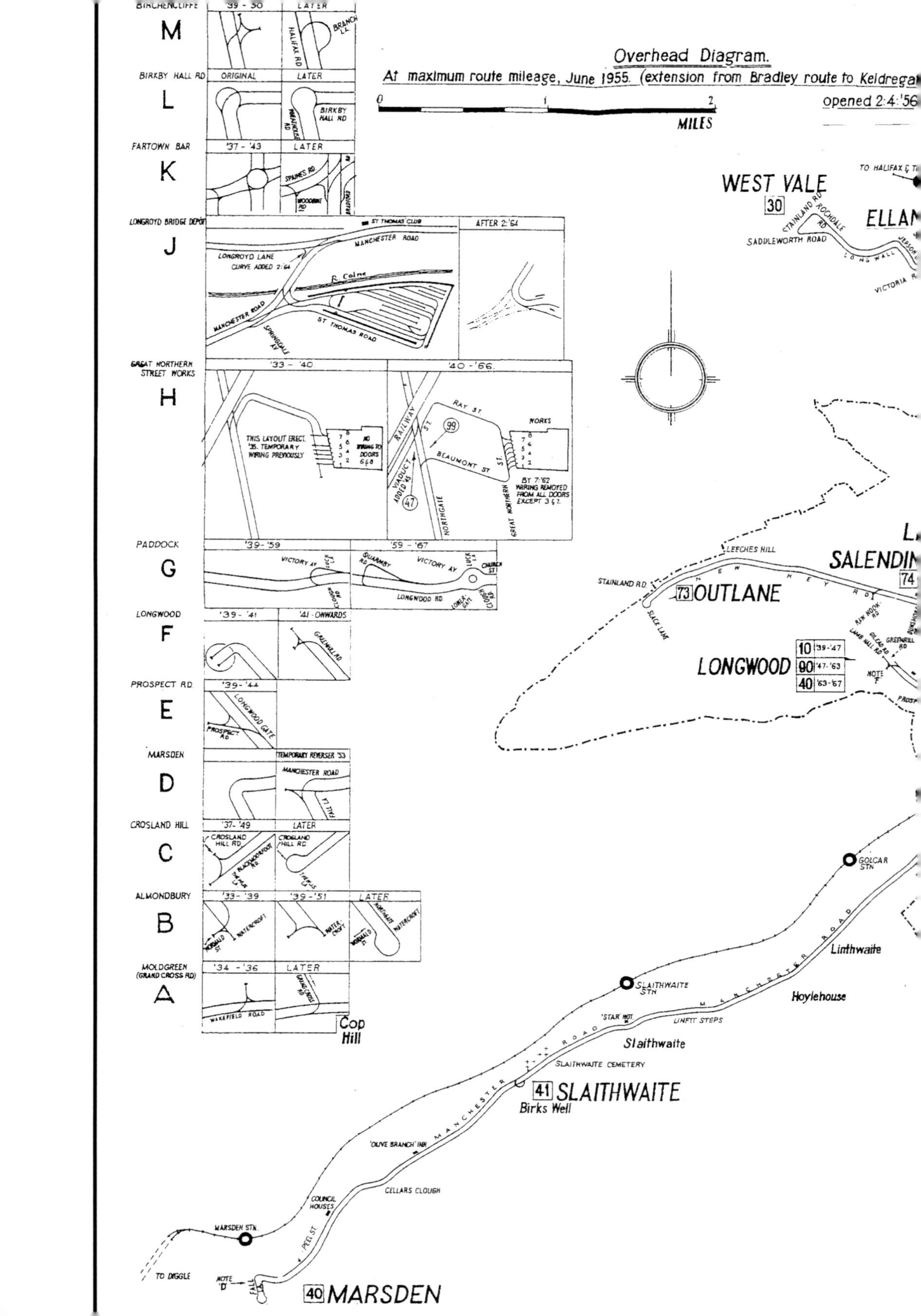

Overhead Diagram.
At maximum route mileage, June 1955. (extension from Bradley route to Keldregat
opened 2:4:'56
MILES
BIRCHENCLIFFE
M
BIRKBY HALL RD
ORIGINAL
LATER
L
FARTOWN BAR
'37 - '43
LATER
K
LONGROYD BRIDGE DEPOT
J
ST THOMAS' CLUB
AFTER 2:'64
MANCHESTER ROAD
LONGROYD LANE
CURVE ADDED 2:'64
R. Colne
ST THOMAS ROAD
SPRINGDALE AV
GREAT NORTHERN STREET WORKS
H
'33 - '40
'40 - '66
THIS LAYOUT ERECT. '35. TEMPORARY WIRING PREVIOUSLY
NO WIRING TO DOORS 6&8
RAILWAY
VIADUCT ADDED '45
RAY ST
BEAUMONT ST
NORTHGATE
GREAT NORTHERN ST.
WORKS
BY 7:'62 WIRING REMOVED FROM ALL DOORS EXCEPT 3 & 7.
PADDOCK
G
'39 - '59
'59 - '67
VICTORY AV
QUARMBY RD
CHURCH ST
LONGWOOD RD
LONGWOOD
F
'39 - '41
'41 - ONWARDS
GREENHILL RD
PROSPECT RD
E
'39 - '44
LONGWOOD GATE
PROSPECT RD
MARSDEN
D
TEMPORARY REVERSER '53
MANCHESTER ROAD
CROSLAND HILL
C
'37 - '49
LATER
CROSLAND HILL RD
ALMONDBURY
B
'33 - '39
'39 - '51
LATER
WATERCROFT
MOLDGREEN (GRAND CROSS RD)
A
'34 - '36
LATER
WAKEFIELD ROAD
GRAND CROSS RD
Cop Hill
TO HALIFAX & T
WEST VALE
30
STAINLAND RD
ROCHDALE RD
SADDLEWORTH ROAD
LONG WALL
VICTORIA
ELLAN
LEECHES HILL
STAINLAND RD.
NEW HEY RD
73 OUTLANE
SLACK LANE
SALENDIN
74
LONGWOOD
10 '39-'47
90 '47-'63
40 '63-'67
NOTE F
GREENHILL RD
LAMB HALL RD
GOLCAR STN
MANCHESTER ROAD
Linthwaite
Hoylehouse
SLAITHWAITE STN
'STAR' HOT.
UNFIT STEPS
Slaithwaite
SLAITHWAITE CEMETERY
41 SLAITHWAITE
Birks Well
'OLIVE BRANCH' INN
CELLARS CLOUGH
COUNCIL HOUSES
MARSDEN STN.
PEEL ST
TO DIGGLE
NOTE 'D'
FALL
40 MARSDEN

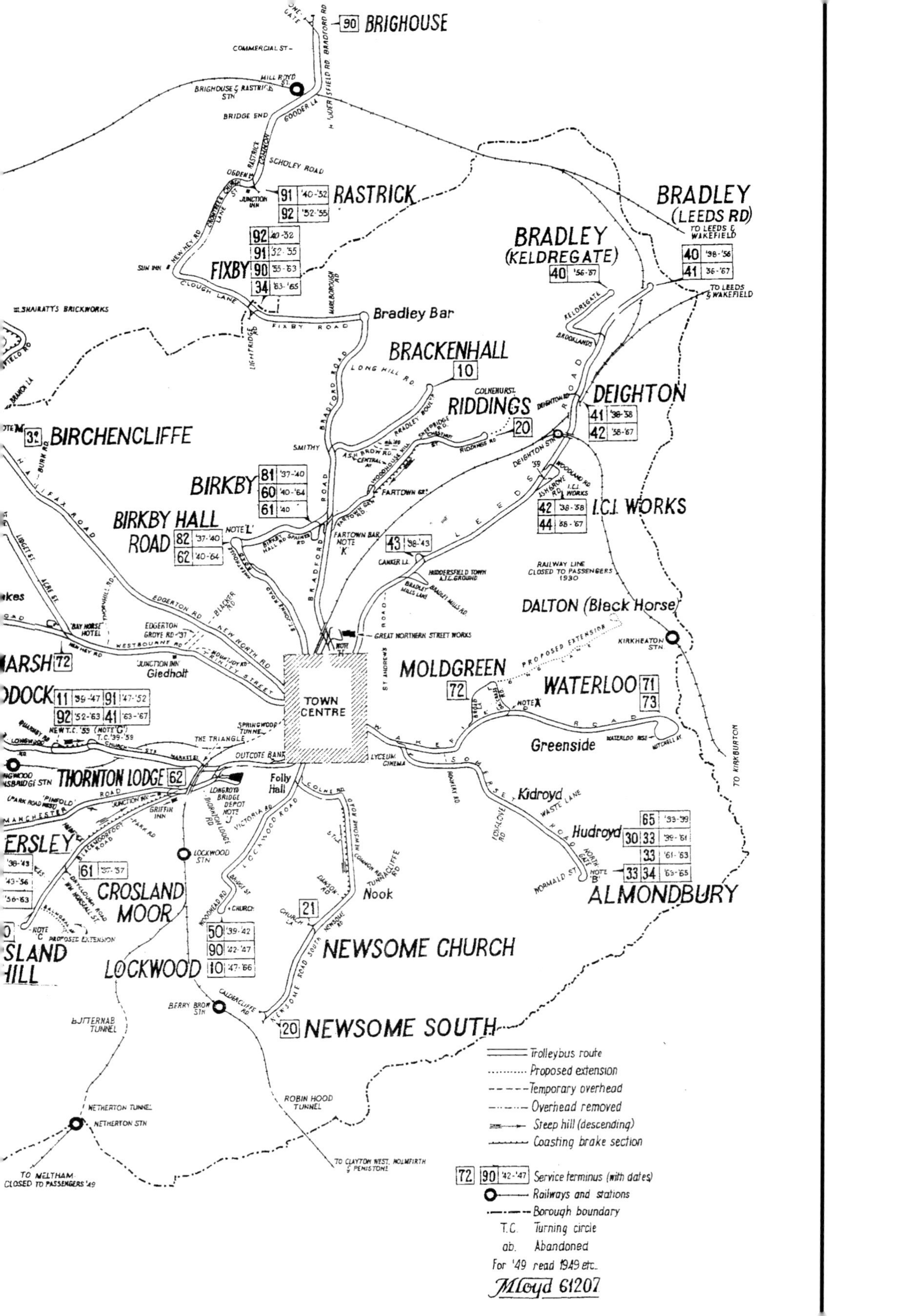
BRIGHOUSE
RASTRICK
FIXBY
BRADLEY (LEEDS RD)
BRADLEY (KELDREGATE)
Bradley Bar
BRACKENHALL
RIDDINGS
DEIGHTON
BIRCHENCLIFFE
BIRKBY
BIRKBY HALL ROAD
I.C.I. WORKS
DALTON (Black Horse)
MOLDGREEN
WATERLOO
Greenside
TOWN CENTRE
THORNTON LODGE
Kidroyd
Hudroyd
ALMONDBURY
CROSLAND MOOR
NEWSOME CHURCH
LOCKWOOD
NEWSOME SOUTH
Trolleybus route
Proposed extension
Temporary overhead
Overhead removed
Steep hill (descending)
Coasting brake section
Service terminus (with dates)
Railways and stations
Borough boundary
T.C. Turning circle
ab. Abandoned
For '49 read 1949 etc.
Mloyd 61207

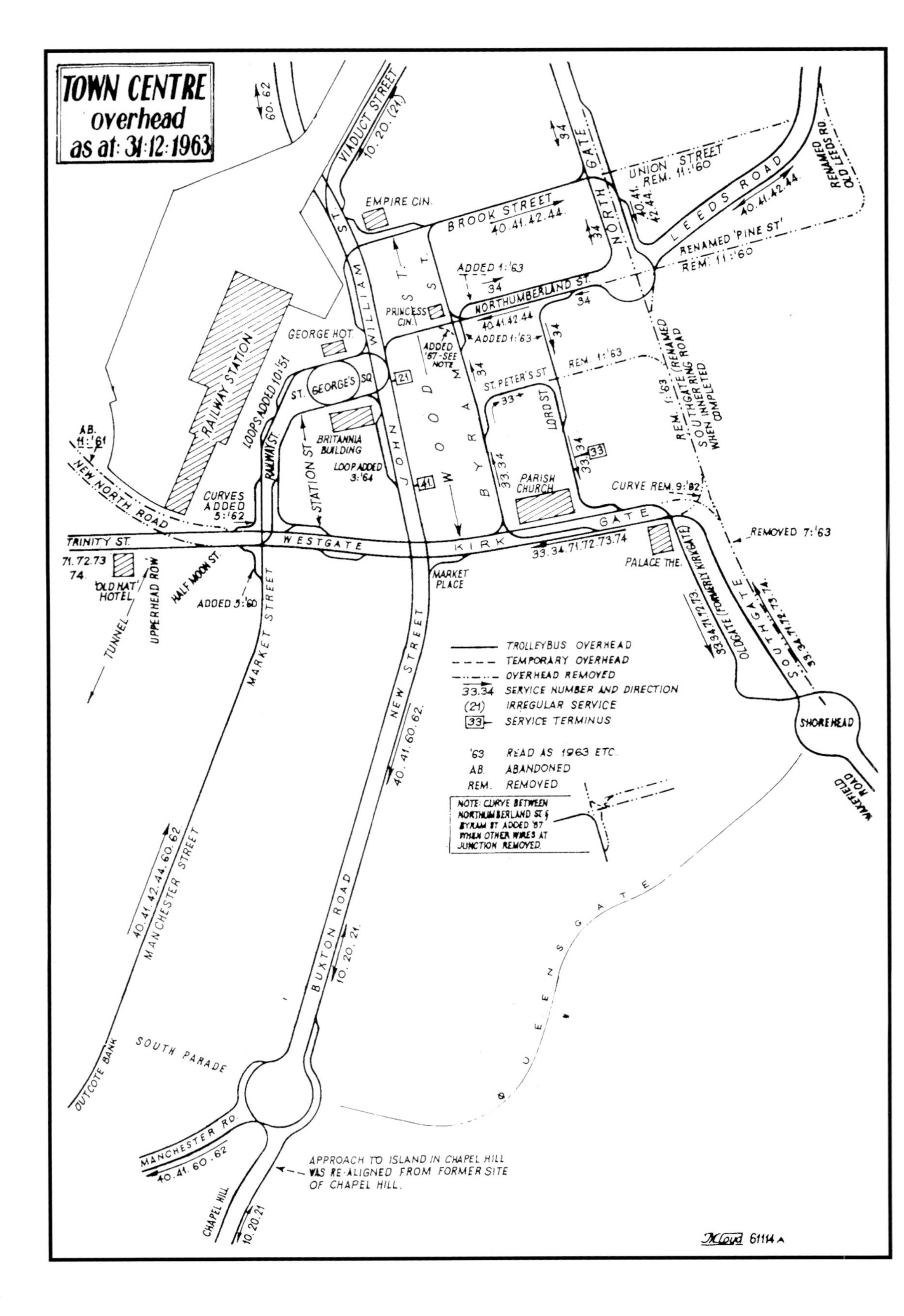
TOWN CENTRE
overhead
as at: 31:12:1963
VIADUCT STREET
10. 20. (21).
60. 62
EMPIRE CIN.
BROOK STREET
40.41.42.44.
NORTH GATE
UNION STREET
REM. 11:'60
LEEDS ROAD
40.41.42.44.
RENAMED OLD LEEDS RD.
RENAMED 'PINE ST'
REM. 11:'60
ADDED 1:'63
NORTHUMBERLAND ST.
PRINCESS CIN.
GEORGE HOT.
ADDED '67-SEE NOTE
ADDED 1:'63
ST. GEORGE'S SQ
ST. PETER'S ST
REM. 1:'63
LORD ST
RAILWAY STATION
LOOPS ADDED 10:'51
RAILWAY ST.
BRITANNIA BUILDING
STATION ST
LOOP ADDED 3:'64
JOHN
WILLIAM ST.
WOOD ST.
BYRAM ST.
PARISH CHURCH
REM. 1:'63
SOUTHGATE (RENAMED SOUTHERN INNER RING ROAD WHEN COMPLETED
CURVE REM. 9:'62
AB. 11:'61
NEW NORTH ROAD
CURVES ADDED 5:'62
TRINITY ST.
WESTGATE
KIRKGATE
33.34.71.72.73.74
PALACE THE.
REMOVED 7:'63
71.72.73 74.
'OLD HAT' HOTEL
UPPERHEAD ROW
HALF MOON ST.
ADDED 5:'60
MARKET PLACE
TUNNEL
MARKET STREET
NEW STREET
OLDGATE (FORMERLY KIRKGATE)
33.34.71.72.73.
SOUTHGATE
33.34.71.72.73.74.
SHOREHEAD
WAKEFIELD ROAD
TROLLEYBUS OVERHEAD
TEMPORARY OVERHEAD
OVERHEAD REMOVED
33.34 SERVICE NUMBER AND DIRECTION
(21) IRREGULAR SERVICE
33 SERVICE TERMINUS
'63 READ AS 1963 ETC.
AB. ABANDONED
REM. REMOVED
NOTE: CURVE BETWEEN NORTHUMBERLAND ST & BYRAM ST ADDED '67 WHEN OTHER WIRES AT JUNCTION REMOVED.
40.41.60.62.
40.41.42.44.60.62.
MANCHESTER STREET
BUXTON ROAD
10.20.21.
QUEENSGATE
OUTCOTE BANK
SOUTH PARADE
MANCHESTER RD.
40.41.60.62
CHAPEL HILL
10.20.21
APPROACH TO ISLAND IN CHAPEL HILL WAS RE-ALIGNED FROM FORMER SITE OF CHAPEL HILL.
61114 A

CONVERSION FROM TRAMS

1. The trolleybus era in Huddersfield began in December 1933 with the commencement of trolleybus operation on the Almondbury route. The town terminus for this was in Byram Street near the Parish Church. One of the initial experimental batch of trolleys, Karrier E6/Park Royal no. 3 stands in Byram Street shortly after entering service. The Almondbury stand remained here for almost thirty years until January 1963, when the stop was moved into Lord Street. The route itself closed in July 1965. Note the lettering on the pole beside the vehicle - 'Trolley Vehicles Start Here'. (Travel Lens Photographic)

2. This view of Huddersfield's main street (John William Street) during the tram / trolleybus changeover was taken in late 1937/early 1938. It shows open balcony tram 109 having just arrived from Dod Lea (Longwood). On the left a Newsome trolleybus is just departing, and on the right the recently introduced Birkby trolleybus (showing the short lived service number 81) is loading alongside Britaninia Buildings. Compare this view with photograph 86 - a similar viewpoint taken almost 30 years later. (Travel Lens Photographic)

BRIGHOUSE AND FIXBY

3. The Brighouse route was service 90 and initially operated to St. George's Square only. During the war it was joined as a through service to Lockwood and from 1947 was linked with the Longwood service. This is Bradford Road, Brighouse, where the service terminated at the junction with Bonegate next to the Ritz cinema. Here, Karrier MS2 / Park Royal no. 564 prepares to reverse into Bonegate on 10th April 1954. This vehicle was rebuilt with a new East Lancs body in 1957. (See cover photo.) The main road to Huddersfield through Brighouse is in the background. This was the nearest point that Huddersfield's trolleybuses got to Bradford, and plans for a through service never came to fruition. (J.Copland)

4. The Brighouse service did not take the direct road to Huddersfield but diverted via Rastrick and Fixby. At Rastrick Common there was an intermediate turning triangle at the junction with Ogden Lane near the Junction Inn. This was not in common use but was allocated service 91. Sunbeam MS2/Park Royal no. 590 passes around 1953. This trolley was one of this type that was never rebuilt, though its body was altered in appearance in the early 1960s (see photograph 83). It was withdrawn in July 1965. Note that the tram track is still in situ over 12 years since the last tram ran. (Roy Brook)

5. At the Borough Boundary at Fixby, another reversing point was provided at Lightridge Road. This was allocated service 92 and there were scheduled journeys turning here. From 10th July 1955 the route beyond this point was abandoned and Fixby became the terminus of service 90. This situation lasted until 1963 when the route was linked to the Almondbury service and given the number 34. The Fixby route was abandoned entirely after Wednesday 14th July 1965. This view shows Sunbeam MS2/Park Royal no. 570 passing Fixby towards Brighouse about 1953. This vehicle was rebuilt with a new East Lancs body in 1957. (Roy Brook)

LONGWOOD
FARTOWN PADDOCK
90
590
ECX 190
BRIGHOUSE
FARTOWN PADDOCK
90
570
ECX 170

6. Between Fixby and just north of Smithy, the tram service ran on a private reserved sleeper track away from public roads. The replacement trolley service ran via Bradley Bar, where the direct road from Brighouse (Bradford Road) was rejoined. A turning circle was provided here during the war (originally allocated service 93). There were no scheduled turns here until 1960, when a secondary school was opened nearby in Bradley Road. At school times special trolley journeys were then provided which turned here. In 1964 frogs were erected in the overhead possibly to allow a complete circle around the roundabout so that the no. 34 service trolleys could turn here and set down schoolchildren at the correct side of the road, then continue the journey to Fixby via the new connection. These frogs were never connected up but remained in situ until the route closed. No. 591, one of the 'hybrid' Sunbeam MS2s rebuilt in 1963 with secondhand East Lancs bodies (in this case originally from no. 561) is seen arriving at Bradley Bar on school special duty together with BUT 609, which at this time (early 1965) was the last trolley to carry a front bumper. One of the unconnected frogs can be seen above 609's roof. (S. Ledgard)

7. In later years the Fixby service, which served a largely affluent area of the town, was infrequent and outside peak hours ran on a basic 30 minute frequency. At Smithy the route joined the much more frequent Brackenhall service. BUT no. 607 is seen negotiating the junction shortly before the Fixby route closed. The Brackenhall route branches off to the right along Ashbrow Road. The route number shown is incorrect and should be 34. Note the loop of span wire hanging on the traction pole. These often appeared just before a route abandonment and were used in connection with overhead wire removal. (S.Ledgard)

BRACKENHALL

8. The original trolley service (10) on Ashbrow Road ran along its full length to the junction with Woodhouse Hill at Sheepridge which had been the tram terminus. (See photograph 11). From there the trolleys were extended down Woodhouse Hill through Fartown Green to Fartown Bar to form a circular loop. New Council housing development in the area resulted in this loop being split and the final half mile of the Sheepridge trolley service was abandoned. The remainder was extended along the new estate road, Bradley Boulevard, into Brackenhall estate from 6th March 1949. The Woodhouse end of the service was extended into the Riddings estate (see Riddings section). The Brackenhall terminus was at a specially constructed turning circle at the end of Bradley Boulevard. Rebuilt Karrier E6 540, numerically the last pre-war trolley, is seen leaving the terminus bound for Lockwood, the service to which the Brackenhall route was linked to throughout its life. (R.F.Mack)

9. Having passed Smithy junction, the route into the town centre followed Bradford Road through the district of Fartown and the major trolleybus junction at Fartown Bar. On Saturday 8th February 1964 BUT no. 613 is passing Graham's Fields on Bradford Road approaching Fartown Bar. This road became a dual carriageway in the early 1970s. (R.F.Mack)

RIDDINGS

10. Originally part of the Woodhouse/ Sheepridge circular route, service 20 was extended into the Corporation housing estate at Riddings on 6th March 1949. The purpose built turning circle is shown here with Sunbeam MS2 / Park Royal no. 588 leaving for Newsome South. This trolley was never rebuilt but latterly did have modernised front destination indicators as shown here. It lasted until July 1965. (S.Ledgard)

11. This is the Ashbrow Road terminus of the Sheepridge / Woodhouse circular route as seen on the last Sunday that trolleys operated on this section of Ashbrow Road. From 6th March 1949 the routes were extended and split to serve Brackenhall and Riddings. Karrier MS2 / Park Royal 548 stands at the terminus before departing to Newsome and will turn right down Woodhouse Hill. Opposite is a pre-war E6 on service 10 to Lockwood running into town via Smithy. Note the tubular suspension of the wiring in Ashbrow Road, with a full width metal tube between the traction poles. This method of wiring suspension was common on the original installation of the system. (Roy Brook)

12. Woodhouse Hill was the steepest gradient on the system (maximum gradient 1 in 8.3/12%). Strict Ministry of Transport rules of operation applied here, and inbound from Riddings trolleys had to engage the coasting brake at the top of the hill for the full descent. This limited the speed of the vehicle to about 15 mph/ 24km/h. At the narrowest part, trolleys were forbidden from passing each other and the relevant traction poles were marked SLW (for Single Line Working). Sunbeam S7 631 is seen near the bottom of the hill descending on the last evening of trolley operation, Wednesday 13th July 1966. This vehicle was purchased for preservation upon withdrawal in 1968 and is kept in working order at the Sandtoft Trolleybus Centre near Doncaster. (J.T.Longbottom)

13. At the bottom of Woodhouse Hill, a turning loop was erected during the war around a small garden area so that, in snow or icy weather, trolleys could be turned when passage up the hill was impossible. The loop was denoted as Fartown Green on destination blinds. There were never any scheduled turns here and the facility would only come into use on one or two days each winter. For this reason it was almost a 'must' that enthusiasts' tours of the system would include a visit around these wires. On such a duty, Karrier MS2 549 stands in the loop on Sunday 24th May, 1964, whilst, on the right, Sunbeam MS2 590 reaches the bottom of Woodhouse Hill on a normal service 20 working. It will come to a halt here to allow the driver to disengage the coasting brake. (J.S.King)

20
NEWSOME SOUTH
ECX 173
C.C. BARNES LTD
UPHOLSTERY WORKS
PHONE HUDD 7065
10
LOCKWOOD
562

14. The Riddings service joined the Fixby / Brackenhall services at Fartown Bar. Approaching the junction from Fartown Green Road is rebuilt Sunbeam MS2 no. 573. Local landmarks are Percy Keep's garage on the right and Lochhead's grocery shop on the left. Notice the stop signs on the traction pole on the extreme left. Trolley stops were generally painted on the pole in yellow with black lettering. Stop plates were used where these were affixed to shelters. The white stop plate here denotes a 'petrol' bus stop. On common sections of route, trolley services were protected by fares cheaper than those on 'petrol buses'. (R.F. Mack)

15. Fartown Bar was the location of the most complex wiring junction outside the town centre. As well as being the junction of the Brackenhall / Fixby and the Riddings services, there was a connection to the Birkby route via Spaines Road. At first there was a complete circle of wires here which all trolleys had to negotiate. This circle also served as the terminus of the Birkby service which was originally intended to work across the junction through to Woodhouse. Apart from some Sunday morning journeys, this never happened and during the war the circle was replaced by more conventional wiring, whilst the Birkby trolleys were provided with other turning arrangements in Spaines Road away from Fartown Bar. The Birkby connecting wires then saw regular, if infrequent, daily use. Late night journeys on service 10 operated to and from Brackenhall via Birkby and latterly there was also a single daily school special journey for Salendine Nook Schools, but the most intensive use was on Sunday mornings when the half hourly service 10 trolleys all operated via Birkby up to 2 pm. This view shows rebuilt Karrier MS2 no. 562 taking the Birkby connecting wires at Fartown Bar and turning into Spaines Road on its journey to Lockwood. Note the 'Lockwood via Birkby' destination provided specifically for these runs. The date is Sunday, 2nd February 1964, the last Sunday that these workings were trolley operated. Although out of view here, there was also a connection from the town centre direction left into Spaines Road that was used by Football Specials to the rugby ground in Spaines Road. (V.Nutton)

16. The Bradford Road routes approached the town centre through the viaduct carrying the railway to Leeds. Originally trolleys were routed straight on into Northgate but from 1945 were diverted right immediately through the viaduct to run parallel with this structure up Viaduct Street. The Northgate wires were retained to allow access to the Great Northern Street Works, the frogs for which are visible through the arch. From January 1963 the Northgate wires came back into service use when the Fixby service, renumbered 34, was re-routed in the town centre to enable it to work through to Almondbury. One further point of note here is the railway crossing denoted by the road sign on the left. This referred to the gas works railway which crossed the junction (diagonally behind the trolley) and ran down Beaumont Street to the gasworks at Leeds Road. The trains were worked by 0-4-0 saddle tank locomotives and ceased operation in 1966. Underneath the arch is trolley 553, a Karrier MS2 (rebuilt with East Lancs body in 1955) on service 34. (S.Ledgard)

R 91824

HUDDERSFIELD CORPORATION PASSENGER TRANSPORT DEPARTMENT

SHEEPRIDGE — No. 10

Thursday, Nov. 28th, 1946, until further notice

FROM TOWN TO SHEEPRIDGE.	FROM SHEEPRIDGE.
MONDAY to FRIDAY.	
5.36 a.m. and every **12** min. until **4.48** p.m.	**5.54** a.m. and every **12** min. until **4.54** p.m.
5.5 p.m. ,, **7½** ,, **6.13** p.m.	**5.10** p.m. ,, **7½** ,, **6.10** p.m.
6.24 p.m. ,, **12** ,, **11.0** p.m.	**6.18** p.m. ,, **12** ,, **11.18** p.m.
***11.25** p.m., ***11.55** p.m.	***11.40** p.m., ***12.10** a.m.
SATURDAYS.	
5.36 a.m. and every **12** min. until **11.48** a.m.	**5.54** a.m. and every **12** min. until **12.06** p.m.
11.59 a.m. ,, **6** ,, **6.35** p.m.	**12.17** p.m. ,, **6** ,, **6.47** p.m.
6.35 p.m. ,, **7½** ,, **11.5** p.m.	**6.55** p.m. ,, **7½** ,, **11.17** p.m.
***11.25** p.m., ***11.55** p.m.	***11.40** p.m., ***12.10** a.m.
SUNDAYS.	
	***6.55** a.m., ***8.11** a.m.
***8.25** a.m. and every **30** min. until ***12.55** p.m.	***8.41** a.m. and every **30** min. until ***1.11** p.m.
1.24 p.m. ,, **12** ,, **11.0** p.m.	**1.42** p.m. ,, **12** ,, **11.18** p.m.
***11.25** p.m., ***11.55** p.m.	***11.40** p.m., ***12.10** a.m.

*** VIA BIRKBY**

WOODHOUSE — No. 20

FROM TOWN TO WOODHOUSE.	FROM WOODHOUSE.
MONDAY to FRIDAY.	
5.43 a.m. and every **12** min. until **4.55** p.m.	**5.49** a.m. and every **12** min. until **5.1** p.m.
5.5 p.m. ,, **7½** ,, **6.13** p.m.	**5.19** p.m. ,, **7½** ,, **6.19** p.m.
6.19 p.m. ,, **12** ,, **11.7** p.m.	**6.25** p.m. ,, **12** ,, **11.13** p.m.
11.25 p.m., **11.55** p.m.	**11.40** p.m., **12.10** a.m.
SATURDAYS.	
5.43 a.m. and every **12** min. until **11.55** a.m.	**5.49** a.m. and every **12** min. until **12.1** p m.
12.5 p.m. ,, **6** ,, **6.35** p.m.	**12.13** p.m. ,, **6** ,, **6.49** p.m.
6.35 p.m. ,, **7½** ,, **11.5** p.m.	**6.49** p.m. ,, **7½** ,, **11.19** p.m.
11.25 p.m., **11.55** p.m.	**11.40** p.m., **12.10** a.m.
SUNDAYS.	
6.40 a.m., **7.55** a.m.	
8.25 a.m. and every **30** min. until **12.55** p.m.	**8.44** a.m. and every **30** min. until **1.14** p.m.
1.31 p.m ,, **12** ,, **11.7** p.m.	**1.37** p.m. ,, **12** ,, **11.13** p.m.
11.25 p.m., **11.55** p.m.	**11.40** p.m., **12.10** a.m.

H. MUSCROFT,
General Manager and Engineer.

November, 1946.

BIRKBY

17. The Birkby terminus was situated in Woodbine Road on a one-way loop around quiet suburban streets about 200 yards from Fartown Bar. This loop was constructed in 1938 to cater for storage of football specials during rugby matches at the Fartown ground. When the Fartown Bar circle was discontinued during the war, Birkby trolleys reversed at the junction of Woodbine Road and Spaines Road using the entry wires for the storage loop. After the war the loop came into use for the Birkby service and football specials were latterly stored in Spaines Road. BUT trolley 614 pauses at the terminus in 1963. The number of parked cars on the left would suggest that this view was taken on a match day. Another feature of the Birkby terminus was its proximity to the former Midland Railway goods branch which ran in a deep cutting under Fartown and Birkby. This was situated on the right of this view out of shot. By the early sixties there were still a couple of trip workings on the branch and it was common to see the white steam of the engine (usually an ex-LMS 4F from Mirfield shed) whilst sitting on the top deck of a trolley here. (J.T.Longbottom)

FARE 2D
FOOTBALL G
420

60
CROSLAND HILL

18. An earlier view of Woodbine Road from just after the war shows the Birkby loop when it was used for the storage of football specials. Of interest here is the variety of pre-war stock shown. In front is 1934 Karrier E6/Park Royal originally no. 20 and renumbered with the rest of the fleet in 1942 by having 400 added to its number. It is in post war livery without the cream swoop at the front, unlike the trolley further down the line, a Brush bodied 1934 Karrier which was one of the few of these early vehicles to have the full post war livery applied. The goods line railway cutting is behind the trolleys. (A.J.Owen)

19. The Birkby terminal loop met the outbound wires at the junction of Spaines Road and Wasp Nest Road. The wires being joined here are the direct link from Fartown Bar and used by the service 10 Brackenhall journeys diverted via Birkby (See photograph 17). Apart from the single daily school special, these diverted journeys did not operate via the Birkby terminal loop. Sunbeam S7 no. 632 is seen turning out of Wasp Nest Road en route to Crosland Hill, the service that the Birkby route was linked to for all its trolleybus existence. This view was taken shortly before the trolleys ceased on the route in February 1964. (V.Nutton)

20. The middle portion of the Birkby route, on Birkby Hall Road, was like a roller coaster ride. This feature was locally known as the 'Switchback', a sharp downhill section followed immediately by an equally steep upward climb. Powering up the 'Switchback' towards the junction with Halifax Old Road is rebuilt Karrier MS2 546. On the right is Norman Park and in the distance can be seen the opposite gradient of the 'Swithchback' with a short level section in the bottom of the dip. (J.S. King)

21. At the top of the other side of the Switchback the route turned left into Wheathouse Road to face another fairly steep descent. The wide road junction here allowed for a turning loop which was designated ‘Birkby Hall Road’. There were regular scheduled turns here especially in the evening peak and these were associated with the nearby Hopkinson’s engineering works. A loop was provided down Wheathouse Road to allow works extras to wait clear of the service trolleys. These workings were given the route number 62. Originally the Birkby service was numbered 81 (with Birkby Hall Road workings numbered 82) even though it worked through to the Crosland Hill service 60/61. After a while the service became number 61 and then 60, which was used in later years for the through service. This view in February 1964 shows Karrier MS2 544 about to make the sharp turn into Wheathouse Road and showing the Birkby Hall Road turning loop wiring. 544 was one of the only two of this type that retained the original three aperture destination arrangement throughout its life. (The other was 541). It was the last trolleybus to run to Birkby on the night of 5th February 1964 and was withdrawn at the end of that month. (V.Nutton)

22. At the junction with Blacker Road, Wheathouse Road ran across into St John’s Road. BUT 615 is shown picking up at the Blacker Road stop. The additional pair of wires for the ‘Hopkinson’s’ loop can be seen. These joined the main wires just off the photograph. The Birkby service was always well used and at the busiest times drivers would often drive at crawling pace for the last half mile along St John’s Road into town to enable the conductor to have time to collect all the fares. (S.Lockwood coll.)

BRADLEY

23. The original Bradley terminus was at the junction of Leeds Road and Bradley Road where trolleys turned at the wide road junction. Leeds Road was the main trans-Pennine trunk road (A62). The Bradley service was linked through to Marsden until January 1963 and then to Longwood until abandonment in July 1967. Originally numbered 40 the Leeds Road terminus became service 41 when the branch to Keldregate opened in 1956. Rebuilt Sunbeam MS2 577 waits at Leeds Road terminus in 1961 before departing on a journey to the town centre only. Except for the early years of the Brighouse route, when 'Huddersfield' was shown on inward journeys trolleys never showed 'Huddersfield' or 'Town Centre' as a final destination. 'St George's Square or 'Market Place' always denoted a central terminus. (J.Copland)

40
MARSDEN

40
LONGWOOD
612
GVH 812

24. In April 1956, a short extension was opened, diverting off the Bradley route into new housing centred around a new road called Keldregate. A neat turning circle was provided where Keldregate met Bradley Road. Alternate Bradley service journeys generally operated to Keldregate and Leeds Road termini. The new terminus took the service number 40. This 1960 view shows one of the final quintet of Roe rebuilt Sunbeam MS2s, 580, before departing on the 10½ mile journey to Marsden, one of the longest trolleybus journeys in the country. (C.W.Routh)

25. A study in wiring. In April 1967, BUT 612 pulls across Leeds Road out of Brooklands at the junction of the Keldregate and Leeds Road routes en route across town to Longwood. (Photobus/S.Lockwood)

26. At the junction of Leeds Road and Deighton Road, a reversing triangle was provided. Known as Deighton (pronounced 'Deeton'), its regular scheduled turns had been reduced over the last years of the route and by the last year of all they had ceased altogether. Originally numbered 41, it was later designated 42 or 44. On the last Sunday of operation on the Bradley route, 9th July 1967, the only surviving Karrier trolley, 548, made a farewell tour including the last ever turn at the Deighton reverser. It is seen turning back onto Leeds Road after this manoeuvre. (S.Lockwood)

27. The large ICI works complex on Leeds Road required extra journeys at peak times and a turning loop was provided around Woodlands Road and Ashgrove Road to cater for them. These journeys ran right up to the end of operation. This point was originally known as 'British Dyes'. This rural looking scene on the loop belies the industrial nature of this area. The final BUT in the fleet, 630, is seen in Woodlands Road in October 1965 and despite appearances, is actually working on an enthusiasts' tour. In the distance is the main Huddersfield to Leeds railway line and above it on the skyline is the Riddings housing estate. (Roy Brook)

28. For specials working to Huddersfield Town AFC's ground at Leeds Road, a loop was provided alongside the ground via Bradley Mills Lane and Bradley Mills Road. In later years, when Huddersfield Town's fortunes began to fade, the loop fell out of use and the Canker Lane turning facility was used instead. Sunbeam MS2 577 is seen heading a line-up of trolleys awaiting homebound fans. Note the 'Fare 3d' indication used specially for these workings. (R.Marshall)

29. A few hundred yards further along Leeds Road towards Bradley was situated the other storage facility for football specials. This was the Canker Lane loop around a piece of spare land. In the later days of the system this was the preferred point for storing vehicles during the match and they were shoehorned in as shown. At the front of the queue on this occasion were Sunbeam MS2s 583 and 585. Note the turnout in the wiring to allow trolleys to proceed from here directly towards Bradley. This connection was removed in the late 1950s. Both 583 and 585 were rebuilt with East Lancs bodies in 1962. (Photobus)

30. Inbound trolleys from Bradley entered the town centre on streets separate to outbound workings. In the lower part of Northumberland Street, Karrier 554 waits to cross Northgate en route to the town centre and Marsden around 1954. Note the clearance of housing from the area on the right - the inhabitants were re-housed at the new Brackenhall estate. This area greatly changed with the construction of the Inner Ring Road in the early 1960s and a large roundabout was built here. (Roy Brook)

WATERLOO

31. Waterloo terminus consisted of a 'round the houses' loop via Penistone Road, Mitchell Avenue and Waterloo Rise. Seen turning from Penistone Road into Mitchell Avenue in 1962, is BUT 620. In the background is the County Motors bus garage, in which can be seen one of their new, but ultimately short lived, Guy Wulfrunian buses. The premises were still operational in 2002, serving as the Huddersfield depot of Yorkshire Traction. Note the "fairy lights" attached to the curve of the overhead wiring. These were provided at various locations on the system to be switched on in foggy conditions in order to guide drivers. (J.Copland)

32. The terminal stop was in Mitchell Avenue (having moved from Waterloo Rise in 1953). Rebuilt Karrier MS2 568 rests before a journey to Lindley in May 1962. (S.Lockwood coll.)

33. At the Junction Inn, Moldgreen, a one way loop of wiring branched off Wakefield Road to operate around Broad Lane, Long Lane and Grand Cross Road, rejoining Wakefield Road near Ravensknowle Park. Originally a reverser was provided in Wakefield Road at the junction with Grosvenor Road but this only lasted a short time prior to the loop being constructed in 1936. This was served by route 72 which operated as a separate service through the town centre to Marsh on weekday daytimes including Saturdays. Some of these journeys were extended beyond Marsh to Salendine Nook reverser and numbered 74. After the introduction of a parallel diesel bus service to Dalton, the Moldgreen trolley service lost its importance and scheduled workings were withdrawn in February 1965, although the wiring remained for use until the end of the system. The last of the 1953 batch of BUT's, 618, is seen in Broad Lane on a Saturday morning in May 1964. (J.T.Longbottom)

71
LINDLEY
568
DVH 68

72
MOLDGREEN
618
GVH 818

ALMONDBURY

34. The village of Almondbury is a more ancient settlement than Huddersfield and has a 13th century Parish church and a 16th century Grammar School granted a charter by King James I in 1608 It was served by the first trolleybus route in 1933. Originally a reverser was provided where trolleys drove into Wormald Street and reversed out into Northgate. (see photograph 102) This arrangement was later changed to a reversal into Wormald Street from Northgate. The reverser was replaced in 1951 by this purpose built turning circle, 100 yards further into the village. Originally service 65 and running to the town centre only, the route was joined to the West Vale service in 1939 and renumbered 30 with Almondbury to town centre only journeys taking the number 33. On a Monday washday in 1960, BUT 623 waits before departure to West Vale. Almondbury Parish Church is in the background. C.W.Routh)

35. The route to Almondbury involved a steady climb up Somerset Road from Wakefield Road. Rebuilt Karrier E6 494 tackles the steepest part between Longley Road and Foxglove Road in 1960 with a view over the eastern part of Huddersfield to the right. (C.W.Routh)

36. This is the junction of Somerset Road and Wakefield Road, where the Almondbury and Waterloo services diverged. From 1964 this area was subject to a massive road scheme involving the conversion of Wakefield Road into a dual carriageway. The Lyceum cinema, which stood behind the vehicles in this view, was demolished as part of these works. The wiring at the junction was subject to several changes as the works progressed and inbound trolleys from Almondbury had two separate lines of wiring available according to the state of the works at the time. One of these involved a tight turn onto Wakefield Road on a very narrow piece of carriageway. This is demonstrated here by Sunbeam MS2 600, with a Joint Omnibus Committee diesel bus on the Lowerhouses service turning in the opposite direction. The trolley is working to Fixby, the route to which the Almondbury service was linked in 1963. This view is dated 8th May 1965, nine weeks before the trolley service was abandoned. (S.Lockwood)

30
ALMONDBURY
TELEVISION
494
AVH 494

34
FIXBY
BRADLEY BAR
107
BCX 107B
600
FCX 800

R 68479.

Huddersfield Corporation Passenger Transport Department.

HUDDERSFIELD - ALMONDBURY ROUTE No. 30

(BYRAM STREET) (WORMALD STREET)

REVISED TIME TABLE of Trolley Vehicle Service

(In conjunction with the West Vale Service).

Commencing Sunday, May 28th, 1939, and until further notice.

Monday to Friday.

TO ALMONDBURY—

5-24 a.m. and every 12 minutes until 6-12 a.m. then

6-12 a.m.	,,	6	,,	9-0 a.m.	,,
9-0 a.m.	,,	12	,,	12-0 noon	,,
12-0 noon	,,	6	,,	2-0 p.m.	,,
2-0 p.m.	,,	12	,,	4-0 p.m.	,,
4-0 p.m.	,,	6	,,	5-0 p.m.	,,
5-0 p.m.	,,	5	,,	6-0 p.m.	,,
6-0 p.m.	,,	6	,,	7-36 p.m.	,,
7-36 p.m.	,,	12	,,	11-0 p.m. and 11-6 p.m.	

Extra Journeys—

10-18 p.m.	10-42 p.m.	Daily.	
2-6 p.m.	2-30 p.m.	2-54 p.m.	Fridays only.
3-18 p.m.	3-42 p.m.	7-42 p.m.	Fridays only.
7-54 p.m.	8-6 p.m.	8-18 p.m.	Fridays only.

FROM ALMONDBURY—

5-36 a.m. and every 12 minutes until 6-24 a.m. then

6-24 a.m.	,,	6	,,	9-12 a.m.	,,
9-12 a.m.	,,	12	,,	12-12 p.m.	,,
12-12 p.m.	,,	6	,,	2-12 p.m.	,,
2-12 p.m.	,,	12	,,	4-12 p.m.	,,
4-12 p.m.	,,	6	,,	7-48 p.m.	,,
7-48 p.m.	,,	12	,,	11-12 p.m. and 11-18 p.m.	

Extra Journeys—

10-30 p.m.	10-54 p.m.	Daily.	
2-18 p.m.	2-42 p.m.	3-6 p.m.	Fridays only.
3-30 p.m.	3-54 p.m.	7-54 p.m.	Fridays only.
8-6 p.m.	8-18 p.m.	8-30 p.m.	Fridays only.

Saturdays.

TO ALMONDBURY—

As Monday to Friday until 11-24 a.m. then
11-30 a.m. and every 6 minutes until 11-12 p.m. and 11-20 p.m.

Extra Journeys—

12-15 p.m. 12-27 p.m. 12-39 p.m.

FROM ALMONDBURY—

As Monday to Friday until 11-36 a.m. then
11-42 a.m. and every 6 minutes until 11-24 p.m. and 11-32 p.m.

Extra Journeys—

12-27 p.m. 12-39 p.m. 12-51 p.m.

Sundays.

TO ALMONDBURY—

9-55 a.m. and every 30 minutes until 12-55 p.m. then
1-24 p.m. 1-36 p.m. 1-48 p.m.
1-54 p.m. and every 6 minutes until 10-54 p.m.

FROM ALMONDBURY—

10-10 a.m. and every 30 minutes until 1-10 p.m. then
1-36 p.m. 1-48 p.m. 2-0 p.m.
2-6 p.m. and every 6 minutes until 11-6 p.m.

POST BOXES will be carried on the following Cars :—

From Almondbury ... Monday to Friday ... 9-0 p.m. and 9-12 p.m. Sunday 7-30 p.m.

ISSUED SUBJECT TO CORPORATION BYE-LAWS.

Passenger Transport Offices,
John William Street,
Huddersfield. 'Phone 3581.

H. C. GODSMARK,
Manager.
May, 1939.

NEWSOME

37. On conversion to trolleybuses in May 1937, the Newsome service was extended some distance beyond the tram terminus at Newsome Church. The new terminal point at Caldercliffe Road was denoted as 'Newsome South', this being a descriptive rather than a geographical indication. Trolleys turned here by reversing into Caldercliffe Road, as shown by Karrier MS2 545 in 1955. Note the studs in the roadway to assist drivers in this manoeuvre. The service was linked through to Riddings, although on this occasion the vehicle is displaying the former terminus 'Woodhouse' which applied before the Riddings extension opened in 1949. In 2002 this area had been subject to traffic calming with speed humps and a mini-roundabout is situated at this junction. (C.W.Routh)

21
ST GEORGES SQ
634
PVH 934
SPECIAL
L
ECX 178

38. The tram terminus at Newsome Church became an intermediate turning point for trolleys, and a regular timetabled service was scheduled to turn here during the day on weekdays. Sunbeam S7 634 is seen at the apex of the reverser and is ready to pull forward into Newsome Road to return to the town centre. (S.Ledgard)

39. The climb to Newsome was long and steep. Descending trolleys were required to use the coasting brake for the steepest section between Dawson Road and Stile Common Road. Seen ascending the hill is rebuilt Sunbeam MS2 578 on driver training duties with a panoramic view of Huddersfield in the background. (S.Ledgard)

40. Newsome Road descended to river level, crossing the River Colne, and then the route turned into the very industrial Colne Road area. Sewer works in 1955 necessitated the use of 'wrong wire working' and special crossovers were inserted into the wiring to allow this. Newly rebuilt Karrier MS2 555 negotiates the obstruction during this period. (Roy Brook)

LOCKWOOD

41. The tram service through Lockwood ran along the Holme Valley through Berry Brow to Honley. Between Lockwood and Berry Brow, the road passed under a railway bridge at the eastern end of Lockwood Viaduct, which carried the former Lancashire and Yorkshire line to Holmfirth, Clayton West and Penistone. This bridge was too low for the passage of trolleybuses and the Honley service passed to Joint Omnibus Committee motorbuses, with trolleybuses running as far as Lockwood only. This remarkable view shows one trolleybus that did pass under the offending bridge. In March 1950, the body of 497 was sold to a farmer near Holmfirth and the stripped body, still on its chassis was towed to its new home via Honley. The tightness of the gap between the body roof (without trolley gear) and bridge is evident. The body was removed on site and the chassis returned for rebuilding with a new Roe body shell. The completed rebuilt vehicle re-entered service in December 1950. (J.P.Senior)

→

42. The terminus at Lockwood was a turning circle located on an awkward site just off the main road alongside Lockwood Church. Originally numbered service 50 and running to the town centre only, the Lockwood route was linked through to Brighouse during the war as service 90. At the 1947 route reorganisation the service was again renumbered to 10 and linked through to Sheepridge. Rebuilt Karrier MS2 554 can be seen negotiating the narrow access road with the turning circle just visible in the left background. The circle still remained in 2002, but the terrace of houses has been demolished. (S.Ledgard)

→

43. This is a damp day in September 1954 in Bridge Street, Lockwood with Karrier MS2 561 picking up passengers at the stop on the bridge over the River Holme. Note the typical Huddersfield police box on the right and the mills at Newsome on the skyline. Despite being bound for Brackenhall, 561 is displaying the old destination 'Sheepridge' which was superseded in 1949. (J.Copland)

10
BRACKENHALL
FARTOWN
554
DVH 54

SHEEPRIDGE
FOLLY HAL
10
561
DVH 61

44. The junction of the Newsome and Lockwood routes was at the bottom of Chapel Hill, just outside the town centre. BUT 607 is seen here en route for Lockwood on a Sunday morning in March 1956. Behind is Sunbeam MS2 603 on service 20, which will operate the automatic frogs to turn into Colne Road. (Roy Brook)

CROSLAND HILL

45. Crosland Hill terminus was in a turning circle at the end of a steady climb up Blackmoorfoot Road. Originally a triangular reverser was provided here but this was replaced by the circle in 1950. Crosland Hill was home to stone quarries, the Huddersfield airstrip and also where Standard Fireworks were made. Amongst the quarry cranes is BUT 626. Rebuilt Karrier E6 493 is operating the first enthusiasts' tour of the system on 1st October 1961. 626 was one of the vehicles put into storage following the conversion of the West Vale route in November 1961 and it re-appeared in October 1962. (Travel Lens Photographic)

Uh22222

HUDDERSFIELD C.P.T.

4d

Issued subject to Bye-laws and Regulations

ORD.

Bell Punch Co., Ltd., London

46. The only relatively level part of the Crosland Hill route was this stretch of Blackmoorfoot Road a few hundred yards before the terminus. On a sunny day in August 1961, rebuilt Sunbeam MS2 576 approaches the terminus, its destination blind already set for the return journey to Birkby. This vehicle was one of those with a Roe body which had its front bumper removed producing a "mini-skirt" look. Behind 576 is the junction with Balmoral Avenue, along which a route extension was authorised, but which was actually opened as a diesel bus route in October 1962. (J.Copland)

47. The tram service terminated at Crosland Moor (Dryclough Road), and a triangular reverser was provided for trolleys which continued to turn short here. There were regular scheduled turns here up to the late 1940s, after which such duties declined until by 1957 there were no trolleys turning here. However, the reverser did remain available for use until the whole route was abandoned in February 1964. Sunbeam MS2 593 turns on the reverser during an enthusiasts' tour on 3rd November 1963. When new in 1950 593 was exhibited at the Commercial Motor Show and had gold lining, red front bumper and wheels, and light coloured upholstery. By 1963, apart from some of the non-standard seat covers in the lower saloon, all these features had been changed. (Travel Lens Photographic)

48. Between Crosland Moor and the Griffin Inn, where the Marsden wires diverged, the gradient was steep enough for a section where the coasting brake was obligatory for descending vehicles. Sunbeam MS2 598 arrives at the junction with Manchester Road. A tight turning circle was provided as shown and trolleys turning here showed "Thornton Lodge" and service number 62. The circle was erected near the end of the Second World War and it was used by trolleys at peak hours. The Marsden wires formerly proceeded along the A62 on the right but the route had been abandoned by the time of this photograph. (S.Lockwood coll.)

MARSDEN

49. The 7½ mile/12km Marsden Route followed the A62 trans-pennine trunk road along the Colne Valley on the opposite side to the Huddersfield to Manchester railway. Marsden was the last settlement before road and rail tackled the Pennines via Standedge into Lancashire. The trolley terminus was in Fall Lane, off the main road, and rebuilt Karrier MS2 557 is seen turning here in June 1957 with typical Pennine backdrop. (J.Copland)

50. Leaving Marsden on its 10½ mile/16km trip through Huddersfield to Bradley is rebuilt Karrier MS2 564. The scenery of mills and hills continued along the Colne Valley most of the way. This area is now familiar as the location for many scenes in television programmes such as "Last of the Summer Wine" and "Where the Heart is". (R.F.Mack)

51. The 41 service to Bradley Leeds Road terminus turned at Slaithwaite (Birks Well) using a purpose built turning circle cut out of the hillside beside the main road. Sunbeam MS2 603 is seen here during the last days of the route, which occurred in the midst of one of the worst winters of the 20th century, January 1963. 603 was unique in that its front bumper incorporated four full length chrome strips. (V.Nutton)

52. Just inside the Huddersfield Borough boundary was a 'round the houses' turning loop at Cowlersley. There were regular scheduled turns here at peak hours, Sunday mornings and late at night. Amongst the snow and ice in Pickford Street is rebuilt Karrier MS2 561. This trolley would donate its body to Sunbeam MS2 587 in 1963 when the chassis was scrapped. (V.Nutton)

53. A view of the Griffin Inn junction of the Marsden and Crosland Hill routes. Pre-war Karrier E6 538 has just negotiated the automatic frogs en route to Marsden. The bridge carries the railway to Penistone ,Holmfirth, Meltham and Clayton West and the line boasted a weekdays named through train to London Marylebone, the "South Yorkshireman" as well as a Saturdays only through train to Poole in Dorset. (Roy Brook)

LONGWOOD

54. The conversion of the Longwood tramway to trolleybuses posed a problem as there was no suitable space for turning at the terminus, (which was always referred to as "Dod Lea" on the trams). The solution made the Longwood trolleybus terminus one of the trolleybus wonders of Britain. A substantial concrete platform was built out from the road some 30 feet over a field and a turntable incorporated. The only other example of a turntable at a public terminus was at Christchurch on the Bournemouth Corporation system. The turntable came into use in January 1939, but was short lived as difficulties in turning vehicles during the wartime blackout resulted in a conventional reversing triangle being adopted. The platform, with its locked turntable plate remained in use for trolleys to reverse onto for the whole life of the trolley service. This photograph was taken just after the route opened and shows the driver in the act of pushing the plate round. (Travel Lens Photographic)

35S 7679

1D

TrolleyBus Ticket

HUDDERSFIELD CORPORATION TROLLEYBUSES.

Issued subject to Bye-laws. Available only on line of route on which issued, and from stage indicated by punch-hole. Must be shown or given up to any servant of the Corporation when required. NOT TRANSFERABLE.

1, 2, 3, 4, 5, 6, 7, 8, 9, 10, 11 TOWN, 12, 13, 14, 15, 16, 17, 18, 19, 20, 21, 22, 23, 24

3, 4, 5, 6, 7, 8, 9, 10, 11 TOWN, 12, 13, 14, 15, 1′, 17, 18, 19, 20, 21, 22, 23, 24, 25, 26

55. This was the way in which trolleys reversed at Longwood for all but the earliest years of the route. Rebuilt Karrier MS2 546 reverses onto the platform on an April evening in 1966. Note that the evening sun has projected a shadow of an overhead frog onto the upper deck side of the vehicle. The Longwood service was linked through to various routes during its life, originally as service 10 to Sheepridge, then from 1947 as service 90 to Brighouse or Fixby and finally from 1963 to Bradley as service 40. (S.Lockwood)

56. This remarkable occurrence took place on 13th February 1967, five months before the route was abandoned. Sunbeam S7 634 was reversing on an early morning journey when the vehicle crashed through the railings, fell off the side of the platform and overturned into the field below. Fortunately the crew was not badly hurt. Recovery was extremely difficult and took place using specialist equipment the following day as seen here. The extensive damage to the vehicle can be seen and it never ran again. In Autumn 1965, 634 had been the last trolley in the fleet to receive a full repaint. (S.Ledgard)

57. The road through Longwood village was quite narrow and this was often cited as the reason that all Huddersfield's trolleys were built to a narrow 7ft 6ins/2286mm wide profile. The use of bracket arms supporting all four wires to save space is also evident in this animated scene showing BUT 629 drawing into a stop to pick up passengers. The loops of span wire hung on the poles indicates that conversion to diesel buses is imminent. (S.Ledgard)

58. The only intermediate turning point on the Longwood route (apart from a short lived reverser at Prospect Road in Longwood Village which was removed during the war) was at Paddock, where regular scheduled turns took place right up to the last day of operation. Originally this was sited at the junction of Church Street and Luck Lane, where a turning loop allowed trolleys to stand without impeding trolleys working in from Longwood. The building of a roundabout here resulted in the turning facility being moved a third of a mile towards Longwood, at the junction of Longwood Road and Quarmby Road. A turning loop at the wide junction with a long lead back to the inbound wires replaced the original turning installation in 1959. This line up headed by Sunbeam S7 636 was unusual, and was due to the temporary curtailing of the Longwood service at Paddock because of the accident to 634 shown in photograph 56. (S.Ledgard)

R 91824

HUDDERSFIELD CORPORATION PASSENGER TRANSPORT DEPARTMENT

LONGWOOD No. 10

Thursday, Nov. 28th, 1946, until further notice

FROM TOWN.	FROM LONGWOOD.
MONDAY to FRIDAY.	
5.31 a.m. and every **12** min. until **4.19** p.m.	**5.54** a.m. and every **12** min. until **4.30** p.m.
4.23 p.m. ,, **7½** ,, **6.23** p.m.	**4.45** p.m. ,, **7½** ,, **6.8** p.m.
6.31 p.m. ,, **12** ,, **11.7** p.m.	**6.18** p.m. ,, **12** ,, **11.30** p.m.
(**11.25** p.m. and **11.55** p.m. to Paddock)	(**11.40** p.m. and **12.10** a.m. from Paddock)
SATURDAYS.	
As Monday to Friday until **10.55** a.m.	As Monday to Friday until **11.30** a.m,
11.6 a.m. and every **6** min. until **7.0** p.m.	**11.39** a.m. and every **6** min. until **6.15** p.m.
7.0 p.m. ,, **7½** ,, **11.8** p.m.	**6.15** p.m. ,, **7½** ,, **11.38** p.m.
(**11.25** p.m. and **11.55** p.m. to Paddock)	(**11.40** p.m., and **12.10** a.m. from Paddock)
SUNDAYS.	
6.30 a.m. **7.45** a.m.	**6.50** a.m. **8.5** a.m.
8.25 a.m. and every **30** min. until **12.55** p.m.	**9.5** a.m. and every **30** min. until **1.5** p.m.
1.19 p.m. ,, **12** ,, **11.7** p.m.	**1.30** p.m. ,, **12** ,, **11.30** p.m.
(**11.25** p.m., and **11.55** p.m. to Paddock)	(**11.40** p.m., and **12.10** a.m. from Paddock)

November, 1946.

H. MUSCROFT,
General Manager and Enigneer.

Alfred Jubb & Son, Ltd., Printers, Huddersfield.

WEST VALE

59. The West Vale terminus was nearer to Halifax than Huddersfield, and the trolleys mixed here with Halifax's green and orange buses, one of which can be seen in the background to this photograph. Rebuilt Sunbeam MS2 576 is at the terminal point in Stainland Road, which was on a one way loop. The West Vale route was linked through to the Almondbury service for the whole of its existence. (Roy Brook)

02046 Qy

HUDDERSFIELD

Issued subject to Bye laws and Regulations.

SINGLE	RETURN
7	

Bell Punch Co., Ltd., London

60. The route between West Vale and Elland included this scenic panorama over the Calder Valley at Hullen Edge. BUT 630 is seen travelling along Long Wall in 1961. Nearer to Elland, the route included a 90 degree bend at the junction of Victoria Road and Jepson Lane. Trolleys were not allowed to pass at this point and automatic light signals, connected to the overhead, were used to ensure this. (J.S.King)

61. This is the first trolley to West Vale and is seen in Elland town centre. There was provision for trolleys to turn here via a 'round the houses loop' which additionally had a facility for vehicles from West Vale to turn back. This connection can be seen trailing in behind the trolley. Karrier E6 114 performed the first run, this being one of the batch with Brush bodies, distinguishable by their bright chromium plated windscreen surrounds. (Travel Lens Photographic)

62. The route between Elland and Huddersfield involved the climb up the Ainleys, a long, twisty and steep ascent which culminated in the road entering a cutting under two high road bridges. BUT 609 is seen at the top of the climb about to pass under one of the bridges with a panorama of Elland in the background. On the steepest part of the descent of the Ainleys towards Elland, trolleys were required to use the coasting brake. (Roy Brook)

63. From the summit of the Ainleys ,the route dropped down towards Huddersfield. At Branch Lane, Birchencliffe, a turning point was provided which had regular peak hour use. Originally a triangular reverser was provided which was unusual in that the trolleys had to cross Halifax Road before reversing into Branch Lane. Around 1950 this arrangement was altered and a turning circle provided. This view shows the original wiring arrangement, with the new turning circle under construction. Note the setted road surface which was commonplace at the time. (J.P.Senior)

64. The West Vale service entered Huddersfield through the district of Edgerton, an area of Victorian affluence. At Imperial Road, seen here, there were reminders of previous transport eras. On the right is one of the waiting shelters erected during the steam tram era of which there were many examples around the town even in the nineteen fifties. This particular one still exists and is in use in 2002. The thin surface reveals the trackwork of a passing loop of the electric tram era. Representing rubber tyred electric transport are BUT 623 and, receding into the distance, Sunbeam MS2 597. (C.W.Routh)

30
ALMONDBURY
623
KVH 223

OUTLANE

65. The village of Outlane is 909 feet above sea level and was the highest trolleybus terminus in Britain during the period that trolleybuses operated here. This bleak scene, taken following a heavy snow shower in December 1967, emphasises the exposed nature of the area. BUT 622 turns across New Hey Road at the terminus. The main road continues over the moors into Lancashire. (Photobus/S.Lockwood)

→

66. In more clement weather, Sunbeam MS2 593 stands at the terminal stop in October 1964. This trolley was overhauled in July /August of that year and lost its front bumper in the process. It did not last long in this form, being withdrawn in July 1965. (J.T.Longbottom)

→

67. The Outlane service was almost a continual climb from the town centre to the summit at Leeches Hill just outside Outlane village. At Salendine Nook, there was a reversing triangle beside the local Co-operative store to which there were regular scheduled turns (numbered 74) right up to the final day of operation. On a quiet sunny day, BUT 629 reverses here. (S.Ledgard)

73
WATERLOO
593
FCX 293
74
KVH 229

68. In 1957, a large campus of three schools was established at Salendine Nook, some distance below the reverser and near the Spotted Cow public house. A purpose built turning loop for trolleys was built to allow school specials to load and unload schoolchildren in safety. This was the only case in Britain where trolleybus turning facilities were provided for the sole use of school specials. Large numbers of specials worked to and from here each schoolday, those in the morning coming through from outside termini via the town centre. As more and more routes were converted to diesel buses, trolley workings were reduced accordingly. The wiring connections to and from the Outlane route are shown here, with school buildings on the right. BUT 628, Outlane bound, drifts across the junctions on a Saturday afternoon in May 1968. On the skyline can be seen Castle Hill with its Jubilee Tower. (Photobus/S.Lockwood)

69. The Marsh terminus was a 'round the houses' loop situated in the junction of the Outlane and Lindley routes. Trolleys entered from the Lindley wires in Acre Street and exited via the inbound Outlane wires in New Hey Road. There were regular services using the loop which were mainly linked through to Moldgreen as service 72. Following the introduction of more diesel bus services in 1965, these services were withdrawn though the wiring remained for emergency use. Rebuilt Karrier E6 532 is seen waiting at the Marsh terminal stop in Gibson Street. (P.Cardno coll.)

LINDLEY

70. The Lindley terminus was another 'round the houses' loop at the end of Lidget Street. Rebuilt Karrier MS2 545 is seen in Thomas Street having just turned off Lidget Street. The vehicle had a short life in its rebuilt state, entering service with its new East Lancs body in April 1961 and being withdrawn prematurely with rear end accident damage in October 1964. (R.F.Mack)

14535 V

HUDDERSFIELD

1½d Issued subject to Bye-laws and Regulations.

SINGLE	RETURN
	10

Bell Punch Co. Ltd., London

71. Having negotiated the terminal loop Lindley trolleys terminated in a lay-by in Lidget Street, though for much of the route's life before the re-development of this side of the street, they had stood just past the public house on the extreme right of the photograph. Sunbeam MS2 596 waits before departing to Waterloo in 1966. (S.Lockwood)

72. A well known landmark in this area is the Lindley Clock Tower in Acre Street which dates from 1899. Karrier MS2 542 calls at the stop here in March 1955. The Lindley route was straight and flat between the terminus and the junction with the Outlane route at Marsh. In addition, the route latterly served the new Huddersfield Royal Infirmary which was opened in Acre Street in the mid 1960s. (J.Copland)

73. The "Bay Horse" junction at Marsh, the point where the Lindley and Outlane routes diverged, is in the background of this view of the lower part of Acre Street. The Marsh turning loop curves to the right into Wellington Street as BUT 620 proceeds towards Lindley. (P.G.Jenkinson)

WATERLOO
71
542
CVH 742

71
620

AROUND THE TOWN CENTRE

74. Our tour starts in Northgate at the junction of Brook Street. Rebuilt Karrier MS2 555 turns right out of Brook Street and pulls across Northgate on a Bradley service prior to turning on to Leeds Road. In the distance BUT 607, inbound from Fixby, comes along Northgate and will turn right at Northumberland Street Roundabout behind the camera to go up Northumberland Street, crossing over the Bradley wires in the process. Prior to October 1960 the Bradley service continued straight across this junction into Union Street. Until the service revisions of January 1963, the wiring in Northgate had not been used for regular services since the diversion of the Bradford Road services via Viaduct Street in 1945. Its main use during this period was for rugby specials to Fartown and access to Great Northern Street Works. By the time of this view, (May 1965) road widening had taken place in connection with the Inner Ring Road scheme. (Photobus/S.Lockwood)

County Borough of HUDDERSFIELD
PASSENGER TRANSPORT DEPT.

SOUVENIR TICKET

Commemorating the end of the Electrical
era of operation of Tramcars and
Trolleybuses.

14th. FEB. 1901 to 13th. JULY 1968

Bell Punch Co., Ltd., London

75. The linking of the Almondbury and Fixby routes in 1963 required considerable additional wiring in the town centre. This is the junction of Byram Street and Northumberland Street with BUT 607 emerging from the former on the half-hourly Fixby service. The eastbound wiring down Northumberland Street was new (westbound being used by inbound Bradley trolleys) and allowed Fixby trolleys access to Northgate and Bradford Road. The connection turning right into Byram Street was used by football specials and peak hour ICI works journeys turning in the town centre. A selection of 1960s cars completes this 1965 scene. (Photobus/S.Lockwood)

76. Football specials to Huddersfield Town AFC ground at Leeds Road loaded at the north end of Byram Street, then turned right into Brook Street joining the Bradley service wires. Rebuilt Karrier E6 532 is seen loading some of the 20,261 supporters who attended a match against Stoke City on 17th March 1962. (Town won 3 - 0!) Note that it is not, on this occasion, showing the 'fare 3d' indication on the route number blind. 532 was one of this type overhauled in 1961. This resulted in having its bumpers removed and producing the 'mini-skirt' look with the front axle in full view. (S.Lockwood)

77. This is Lord Street, which became the location of the town centre Almondbury stop in January 1963 when the service was joined to that from Fixby. New wiring was erected the full length of the street from Northumberland Street to Kirkgate to allow access for trolleys from Fixby. Lord Street was, in effect motorbus territory and most such services from the north and east of the town used it as a terminus. Sunbeam MS2 605 stands on Lord Street's stone setts in May 1964, resplendent after its final overhaul and repaint. It was withdrawn in 1966. (Roy Brook)

→

78. The Waterloo and Almondbury services entered the town centre from Wakefield Road via Southgate. This road was incorporated into the new dual carriageway Inner Ring Road in the early 1960's with a new roundabout being constructed at Shorehead. This scene shows Southgate immediately before these alterations with Karrier MS2's 547 (unrebuilt) and 567 (rebuilt with Roe body in 1958) in evidence. The new building is the Telephone Exchange and the 'Oxford' public house in front of it would shortly be demolished. The outbound wiring, which 547 is using would be abandoned in July 1963 and trolleys diverted along Oldgate to access Wakefield Road at the Shorehead Roundabout. (V.Nutton)

→

79. Taken from the front upper-deck seat of an Almondbury bound trolley, this is a view of Oldgate at 8.15 am one morning in the Spring of 1965. Note the bracket arms supporting the wiring. In the left background is the Shorehead roundabout on the Inner Ring Road. The trolley parked in the lay-by will follow behind to Almondbury then operate the morning special service from there through to Salendine Nook Schools. Note the Ford Anglia behind 587. (J.T.Longbottom)

72
DVH 67
30
ALMONDBURY
547
CVH 747
33

80. King of the Road ? This is Kirkgate at 4.30pm on a typical Friday evening in May 1965. The dominance of the trolleybus is evident. In six weeks' time, however, following the conversion of the Almondbury service to diesel bus operation, the tide will have turned and only the 71 Lindley trolley from all those in view here would remain. BUT 616 is leading, with MS2s 553 and 601 behind, pausing at the trigger to switch on to the parallel wires to take the curve into Byram Street. 553 is a service 33 from Almondbury terminating in the town centre and 601 is operating a tea-time special, working in from Almondbury. It would then use the connecting wires through Byram Street to run to the ICI Works on Leeds Road and pick up workers from there. On the left a trolley (probably 592) is emerging from Lord Street en route to Almondbury. (Photobus/S.Lockwood)

81. Byram Street was the location of the Almondbury queuestand from the first days of the system. It was accessed from Kirkgate where the wiring allowed turns from either direction into Byram Street. After January 1963 when the Almonbury and Fixby services were joined, the Almondbury queuestand was moved into Lord Street and this stop became the main town centre stop for Fixby. The Byram Street wires were also part of the convoluted route followed by trolleys returning to depot from the Outlane, Lindley and West Vale services. This was due to the lack of connecting wires at key junctions, a situation that was not remedied until the last few years of the system. This view shows two BUT vehicles in August 1960, 610 at the Almondbury stop and 615 overtaking on its way around the town centre having finished service from the Lindley direction. At this point it is actually travelling away from the direction of Longroyd Bridge Depot. Note the different arrangement of the chrome strips on each vehicle's front bumper. (C.W.Routh)

82. Trolleys entering the town centre from the south did so via Buxton Road, crossing into New Street at the junction with High Street and Ramsden Street. Karrier MS2 549 is seen at this point in August 1964. Service 40 vehicles working in from Longwood had been routed this way since the closure of the Market Street wires in March of that year. 549 was the only DVH registered vehicle not to be rebuilt and in its last years could be distinguished by the bright surround to its nearside windscreen. It remained in service until February 1965. Today, almost all of the buildings in view, including the Curzon Cinema in the right background, have been demolished and the area is a pedestrian precinct. (J.T.Longbottom)

70
MARKET PLACE
615
GVH 815
30
ALMONDBURY
610
GVH810

40
BRADLEY
549
DVH 49
GJX 771

83. The hub of Huddersfield's trolley system was at the Market Place, where the North - South services from John William Street into New Street crossed at right angles the east - west services from Kirkgate into Westgate. All trolleys in service passed this point except those on the Almondbury service (and later Fixby) which turned into Byram Street just before reaching this junction. With the Market Place in the background, Sunbeam MS2 590 enters John William Street from New Street on a Saturday afternoon in May 1965 All four overhead crossings can be seen. Note also the conductor standing on the lower entrance step in readiness to jump off and pull the trigger for the loop accommodating the Brackenhall and Riddings queuestands. (Photobus/ S.Lockwood)

→

84. John William Street contained the main town centre stops for five of the trolley services. In the southerly direction there were never any loops provided in the overhead wiring to allow overtaking and despite careful timetabling, it was a common sight for trolleys to be queuing patiently and for the trolley booms to be lowered to allow the trolley behind to overtake. This view shows the booms of BUT 608 being replaced after this process. The vehicle is at the Lockwood stop and is working the Sunday morning journeys which operated to and from Brackenhall via Birkby. (Roy Brook)

→

85. Ancient and modern - This interesting view of John William Street looking North dates from the early 1950s and shows two pre-war Karrier vehicles. In front is 470, an unrebuilt vehicle, loading at the Newsome stand. This was withdrawn in 1953, sold to Epsom and Ewell Urban District Council and converted into a mobile toilet for use on Epsom racecourse. It was eventually rescued for preservation and still exists, though unrestored. Waiting behind is 497, a rebuilt version with 1950 Roe body, on the Fixby to Longwood service 90. 497 lasted in service until 1962. On the corner of Northumberland Street behind 497 are the Corporation Transport Offices. (Roy Brook)

10
LOCKWOOD
BIRKBY
HUDDERSFIELD
608
GVH 808

Rees
90
LONGWOOD
497
AVH 497
20
COLNE Rd
470
AVH 470

86. Trolleys in John William Street looking South. After the closure of the Market Street wiring in 1964, journeys from the depot had to use the main New Street/John William Street wires to St George's Square. Sunbeam MS2 604 is seen about to turn into the Square en route to take up service to Outlane. The conductor can be seen pulling the trigger on the pole on the right to allow this manoeuvre. Also in view is the loop in the wiring erected in 1964 to allow trolleys to overtake vehicles loading at the Brackenhall and Riddings queustands from which 597, distinguishable by its bright windscreen surrounds, has just departed. This view was taken on General Election day, 31st March 1966, when the Labour government, led by Huddersfield born Harold Wilson won an increased majority in the House of Commons. (S.Lockwood)

87. A busy scene in Westgate in the late 1950s with trolleys coming up from Kirkgate, having crossed the John William Street / New Street wires. Heading the pack is one of the duo of surviving unrebuilt pre war Karriers ,476, followed by a rebuilt example, 532 on the Marsh service. In the opposite direction post war Karrier MS2 550 with 1958 Roe body proceeds towards Kirkgate where it will turn left into Byram Street to access the Almondbury queuestand. The photograph is taken from the main West Vale stop, for which a loop in the wiring was provided, the frogs for which are visible. On the left is Rushworth's department store, long since closed and a familiar bright green Yorkshire Electricity Board Morris van. (V.Nutton)

88. Near the top of Westgate, the Market Street wires crossed Westgate into Railway Street. In the early 1960s connecting wires were put in from Market Street and Railway Street to allow a much more direct access to the Outlane and Lindley services from the depot, obviating the previous lengthy detour around the town centre. Ill fated Sunbeam S7 634 crosses the junction into Westgate showing the wiring connection to and from Railway Street. Prior to November 1961, the West Vale route diverged to the right up New North Road in front of the large building in the background. The typical road traffic of the time includes a Thames Trader wagon and a Ford Cortina Mark I car. (R.F.Mack)

OUTLANE
476
AVH 476

71
WATERLOO
MOLDGREEN
634
PVH 934
YVH 421
Y W C A

89. During 1947 a diversionary route for all service trolleys entering the town centre from the Manchester Road direction was opened via Outcote Bank, Manchester Street, Market Street and Railway Street to St Georges Square. Sunbeam MS2 593 climbs Outcote Bank from Manchester Road with a trolley replacement diesel bus in 'pseudo' trolleybus livery trailing behind. In the background is a typical Huddersfield industrial landscape around Longroyd Bridge. This routeing lasted until March 1964, when the redevelopment of the town centre caused the remaining Manchester Road service (from Longwood) to revert to the original wiring which had been retained for use by trolleys running into service from the depot. (V.Nutton)

90. At the top of Outcote Bank the road continued into Manchester Street alongside the town's Upperhead Row bus station. Shelters were provided for the trolley services and rebuilt Karrier MS2 with East Lancs body is seen here on 20th August 1955 alongside a Huddersfield Joint Omnibus Services wartime Daimler CWA6 'petrol' bus with lowbridge Duple body. 557 was subsequently withdrawn in 1962 and its body transferred to Sunbeam MS2 587. Manchester Street and this bus station no longer exist, having been swallowed up in the development of the Civic Centre and the Inner Ring Road in the mid to late 1960s. (J.Copland)

91. For three months, between April and July 1939, the main streets of the town (John William Street, New Street and Buxton Road) were closed to traffic to permit complete reconstruction including removal of tram rails. Accordingly, wiring for trolleys was erected in both directions in Market Street, Manchester Street and South Parade to enable services to be maintained across the town centre. Temporary wooden loading barriers were placed in Market Street for southbound services. This rare view shows Karrier E6 62 loading in Market Street near the junction with Westgate loading for Crosland Moor. Following the reopening of the main streets, the southbound wires of the diversion were removed, but those in the Northbound direction in Market Street were mostly retained and eventually brought back into use in October 1947. (P.Cardno coll.)

60
BIRKBY
557
DVH 57
210
CCX700

61

92. Outside the station forecourt in Railway Street, loading stands were provided for the Birkby and Brighouse/Fixby services with a long shelter which caused controversy when erected in 1952. Loops in the overhead wiring were provided to allow Bradley trolleys to overtake en route to their stand outside the George Hotel in John William Street. This view shows the Birkby loading point and the specially decorated trolley, 535, which commemorated the Queen's Coronation in June 1953. It operated in this form in normal service for the period of the celebrations and was then withdrawn for rebuilding with a new Roe body finally being withdrawn in January 1963. (Roy Brook)

→

93. At the other end of the shelter was the Brighouse / Fixby loading point together with an elongated loop in the wiring. This loading point lasted until the Fixby service was re-routed via Byram Street in 1963. Parked just past the stand, receiving attention from overhead line staff, is a rebuilt Karrier/Sunbeam MS2 with Roe body. Huddersfield was meticulous in its maintenance of the overhead wiring and equipment, and trolleys were never seen in service with ragged or bent trolley booms. This trolley is probably having its booms re-taped following a dewirement. The derrick (tower wagon) is one of a pair of AEC Mandator type dating from 1958. In the background is the famous façade of Huddersfield railway station, seen here before the stonework was cleaned. John Betjeman described this as "the most splendid station façade in England". (Photobus)

→

94. St George's Square in the 1950s. This area in front of the station was the main parking provision in the town centre for spare trolleys and it was adjacent to the Transport Department's head office on the corner of Northumberland Street. A complete circle of wires was provided around the main flower beds and this also served as a turning point for trolleys terminating in the town centre. Prior to 1950, when the Square was re-modelled, trolleys were parked at right angles to the later arrangement where there was an unconnected 'siding' wire for spare vehicles. Seen turning amongst the blooms is Sunbeam MS2 598. The traction poles around the Square were painted a beige shade with red bands instead of the usual green. The Lion on top of Lion buildings was still a local landmark in 2002 and legend has it that the it walks around the edge of the building on the stroke of midnight. (Photobus/J.Copland)

DANGER
OVERHEAD
REPAIRS
HUDDERSFIELD
MVH 388

BEATRICE
STEPHENS
598
HUDDERSFIELD
FCX 298

DEPOTS AND WORKS

95. Built in 1887 to house the steam trams, Great Northern Street depot and works was used as a running depot for the first trolleybuses. Most of the older trolleybuses continued to run out of here until they were withdrawn shortly after the War. All heavy repair and overhaul work on the fleet was carried out here throughout the trolleybus era, the last such vehicle to be dealt with being Sunbeam S7 639 which re-entered service after overhaul in June 1966. The frontage of the depot is shown here with 'Tramway Depot' on the stonework. Regretfully, the building was demolished in the 1990's and the site used for a retail outlet. In front of the works in this photograph is trolley 549 during a Sunday enthusiasts' tour. A loop of wiring connected the works to Northgate via Beaumont Street and Ray Street. By the time of this view (1964), the number of wiring connections into the works itself had been reduced to just two. (J.S.King)

96. This glimpse inside Great Northern Street works shows some interesting goings-on. The trolleys on the left are two of the Sunbeam MS2s that were rebuilt with secondhand East Lancashire bodies in 1963. They are shown here during that process with 591 bearing the body from 561, still showing its former fleet number. Beyond is 592, now carrying the body from 563. On the right is a KVH registered BUT undergoing overhaul. (S.Lockwood coll.)

97. The main running depot for the whole of the trolleybus era was situated at St Thomas Road, Longroyd Bridge. Originally the tram depot dating from 1901, the site was extensively rebuilt in 1938 to house the trolleybus fleet. The main entrance / exit is seen in this view. There was a rear exit into St Thomas Road on the right. At the front exit (the right hand doors seen here) was the only remaining example of tubular suspension and this can be seen above the vehicle here. S7 640 on the left is being taken out of service with a defect and replaced by S7 634. The passengers can be seen transferring to 634 to resume their journey to Longwood. The depot subsequently passed to West Yorkshire PTE in 1974 but has since been disposed of. (J.T.Longbottom)

98. The interior of Longroyd Bridge Depot was particularly spacious and light. This early 1960s scene shows how varied the fleet had become. Four examples of Karrier/Sunbeam MS2s can be seen lined up. From the left is 569, rebuilt with Roe body in 1958 and further modified with a 'mini skirt' front dash, then 544 in unaltered condition still with the three aperture front destination arrangement. Thirdly, there is a dusty and unidentifiable ECX registered trolley which is awaiting rebuilding and rebodying with an East Lancs body, and finally 546 rebuilt with an East Lancs body in 1961. (Travel Lens Photographic)

99. BUT 618 receives a wash in the mechanical washer which lowered itself around the vehicle. The lady cleaners shunted the trolleys on to and off the washing area. (S.Ledgard)

ROLLING STOCK

100. **VH 5723**
In April 1933, the Corporation ordered six experimental trolleybuses to assess the best type for future operation. These consisted of four makes of chassis and three body types. This was the first vehicle, a Ransomes D6 with a Brush 60 seat body. It is seen here just before delivery to Huddersfield. Before it entered service the fleet number on the front panel was moved down to allow for the Borough crest to be placed centrally. This vehicle, together with the other five, opened the Almondbury trolley service in December 1933 and remained in use until 1946. Towards the end of the War, it was decorated to celebrate VE day. (R.Marshall coll.)

→

102. **5 VH 5727**
6 VH 5728

The final vehicles of this batch had similar English Electic bodywork with number 5 having a Karrier E6 chassis and number 6 an AEC 663T chassis. These two were different in appearance to the others, having two windows at the front of the upper deck. No. 6 was also unique in the Huddersfield trolleybus fleet by having only one step up to the platform. All other trolleys had a two step entrance - even though in later designs it was not structurally necessary. No. 6 survived until 1946, and no. 5 lasted until 1947. This view of AEC number 6 shows it using the original reverser at Almondbury, having just reversed out of Wormald Street into Northgate. Note the 'Byram Street' destination and the AEC Regal bus of the Joint Omnibus Committee behind. (J.P Senior coll.)

101. **2 VH 5724**
3 VH 5725
4 VH 5726

This trio of vehicles were visually almost identical and all had Park Royal 60 seat bodies. Numbers 2 and 3 had Karrier E6 chassis built in Huddersfield whereas no. 4 had a Sunbeam MS2 chassis. Karrier number 2 had the honour of being the official first trolleybus at the opening of the system on 4th December 1933. This photograph shows number 3 when new, ascending Somerset Road to Almondbury showing the original service number 65. No. 4 was withdrawn in 1943, and the Karriers survived until 1947.
(Karrier Motors Ltd)

→

103. **7 to 18 VH 6750 - VH 6761**

The first bulk orders for trolleybuses occurred in 1934 for the Waterloo to Outlane/Lindley routes. Twenty four vehicles were delivered, all on locally made Karrier E6 chassis but with the body order split evenly, the first 12 being from Brush with the rest from Park Royal. No. 8 is seen here before delivery sporting an experimental form of trafficator on the front panel. These trolleys lasted until 1948, when the whole of this Brush bodied batch was sold to Reading Corporation. Only six actually entered service there including this one, which became 160 in that fleet and ran until 1956/7. (See Trolleybus Classics number 5 - *Reading Trolleybuses*).
(S.Lockwood coll.)

65
SPECIAL

104. **19 to 30 VH 6765, 6767 ,6766 ,6768, 6871, 6872, 6769, 6762, 6770,6773,6763,6764.**

The second batch had Park Royal bodies similar in looks to those of the original experimental vehicles. This is number 19 before delivery. Trolleybuses up to and including number 30 were not fitted with coasting brake equipment and could not therefore operate on those routes where Ministry of Transport regulations required this. In 1940 the body of number 28 was burnt out during fog and its chassis was given a new Park Royal body in the style of the large Park Royal batch to be described later under photograph 107. All of these vehicles were withdrawn during 1948.
(Park Royal Vehicles)

105. **31 VH 8722**

This was a "one off" Karrier E6 with a Weymann all metal body. Because of this it was the only Huddersfield trolleybus not to have traction lighting (ie powered directly off the overhead wires) but used a low voltage motor generator. The vehicle entered service in 1936, lasting until 1949. It is seen here undergoing a tilt test before delivery to Huddersfield. This was carried out at London Transport's Chiswick Works. (Roy Brook coll.)

106. **32 VH 8530**
33 - 40 VH 9933 - 9940

These vehicles were the first manifestations of the standard Huddersfield pre-war trolleybus used to replace the remainder of the tram fleet. The Park Royal bodies seated 64. No. 32 was the prototype and introduced the swooping cream front that characterised all further vehicles. It entered service in 1936 and was the last Karrier trolleybus for Huddersfield that was built in its home town. The remainder, 33 to 40 were delivered in 1937 for the Newsome tram conversion in May of that year. Broadly similar to subsequent Karrier deliveries, the main difference being the three supports to the trolley gantry on the roof rather than two. These vehicles survived until 1949. The photograph shows number 40 when new in St George's Square outside the George Hotel. Note the form of livery of this period (the colours were actually maroon below the lower deck windows and bright red above) with the fleetname 'Huddersfield Transport' on either side of the Borough crest. (R.Marshall coll.)

0 10 20 30 40 50 60 70 80 90
Nº 31

HO
HUDDERSFIELD TRANSPORT
Nº 40
VH 9940

107. **41 - 105 AVH 441 to 505 Park Royal bodies**
106 - 115 AVH 506 to 515 Brush bodies
126 - 140 BVH 126 to 140 Park Royal bodies

This large class of Karrier E6 trolleybuses delivered between October 1937 and early 1939 enabled most of the tram system to be abandoned. All were largely identical, the main differences being: 41 to 48 had divided front dash panels; 106 to 115 had bright windscreen surrounds and 126 to 140 had slightly lower windscreens. This view, taken before delivery, shows 58. Note the way in which the fleet number is shown "No. 58" in gilt figures. (S.Lockwood coll.)

(right)
108. **41 - 115, 126 - 140**

This photograph shows the typical rear profile of the standard pre-war trolleybus. Taken in the early 1950s, it shows the Post Office Red livery introduced in 1941, with 'Huddersfield Corporation' in black letters on the cream band below the lower deck windows. All trolleybuses had their fleet numbers increased by 400 in 1942, and therefore this vehicle was formerly number 88. It appears to have suffered a dewirement. The bracket on the rear panel beside the entrance was for the post box. This was a common feature of the trams but was sparsely used on trolleys and ceased altogether on the outbreak of war in 1939. An indication 'Postal' was included in red on destination blinds. Also of note is the 'Power Petrol' sticker on the rear window. This was carried by most trolleybuses at this time and was one of the few examples of exterior advertising. Presumably Power supplied fuel for the Joint Omnibus Committee's fleet. The first withdrawal of these vehicles was number 504 following accident damage in 1945. Twenty-two of the type were rebuilt between 1950 and 1954 with new Roe bodies. (see photograph 110). The last un-rebuilt examples to remain in service were numbers 476 and 531 which survived until October 1959, almost three years after all the other original examples had disappeared. (V.C.Jones, courtesy Ian Allan Publishing)

(below)
109. **116 - 125**
AVH 516 - 525
This batch of ten Karrier E6s carried Weymann's interpretation of the Huddersfield standard trolleybus style. They were the last pre-war buses to be delivered, entering service in early 1940. Visually they were distinctive due to their exaggerated bulbous front. They also had English Electric electrical equipment instead of the normal Metropolitan Vickers type. Nicknamed 'Messerschmidts' by the crews because of the staccato noise made by the contactors, these vehicles lasted until the early 1950s, the last ones being withdrawn at the time of the Brighouse route abandonment in July 1955. Six were rebuilt with Roe bodies in 1952. Number 516 (ex 116) is seen parked at the junction of Woodbine Road and Spaines Road on Rugby special duties shortly before withdrawal. Note the 'Huddersfield' fleetname which was applied to all trolleybuses from 1953. (A.J.Owen)

110. **Karrier E6 rebuilds**
Between 1950 and 1954, twenty-eight of the pre-war standard vehicles were rebuilt with new Roe 66 seat bodywork following extensive chassis refurbishment. These bodies introduced a modern look to the fleet and had two windows to the front upper deck, revised front destination indicator arrangements, and front and rear bumpers. The first vehicle dealt with, 493, is seen in this rare photograph taken at Newsome South terminus during a test run before entering service in August 1950. The vehicles were dealt with in four batches of seven as shown below and the final fourteen had sliding rather than hinged cab doors. At least 493, and probably the others in the first batch of seven, were delivered from the bodybuilder as shells only in undercoat and were subsequently completed by the Corporation in Great Northern Street Works.

491,492,493,494,497,508,509
475,496,498,499,501,502,503
484,517,518,519,523,524,525
527,528,529,532,535,536,540

The first withdrawals (475, 484) took place in October 1959, although nine (519, 523, 525, 527, 528, 529, 532, 535, 536) were given overhauls between 1960 and 1962 which resulted in their bumpers being removed (see photograph 76). Final withdrawals took place in January 1963 as a result of the Marsden route abandonment. (J.P.Senior)

(right)
111. **541 - 548 CVH 741 to 748**
549 - 568 DVH 49 to 68
569 - 592 ECX 169 to 192
This group of 52 vehicles formed the backbone of post war deliveries and entered service between 1947 and 1949. They had Sunbeam MS2 chassis and Park Royal 70 seat bodies. The CVH and DVH vehicles carried Karrier badges and the ECX group had Sunbeam insignia. The bodies were to a severe styling and retained the old-fashioned three - window arrangement at the front which had been a feature of the pre-war trolleybuses. This view of 574 and 546 in Longroyd Bridge Depot in 1950 shows the detail differences between the Karrier and Sunbeam types. The badges were removed, usually at the vehicles first overhaul. The CVH and DVH batches had a push out opening window fitted to the middle pane of the front upper deck window early in their life. Sunbeams 587 and 592 originally had experimental fluorescent saloon lighting when new but this was removed in 1952. Both the trolleybuses shown here were subsequently rebuilt, 546 with an East Lancashire body in 1961 and 574 with a Roe body in 1959. (A.B.Cross)

(below)

112. **541 - 592**

An example of the rear of these vehicles is shown here. Note the post box bracket was still provided on these vehicles even though it was never used, and the chromed rear bumpers. All but seven of these vehicles were eventually rebuilt with new bodies by East Lancashire or Roe as described in the following photographs. Those never rebuilt were:-541, 542, 544, 547, 549, 588 and 590. Of these, all except 541 and 544 had their front destination arrangements altered in 1960-1961 to the modern two aperture arrangement. Withdrawals of the un-rebuilt vehicles started in February 1964 with 588 and 590 lasting until July 1965. 541 was presented to the National Trolleybus Assocation for preservation and it was brought back to Huddersfield to operate a tour on the final day of trolleybus operation. It is currently about to re-enter service at the Sandtoft Transport Centre after extensive renovation. The vehicle shown here was rebuilt with a new Roe body in 1958 and withdrawn in 1965. (See photograph 114). (A.B.Cross)

113. **Karrier/Sunbeam MS2 rebuilds - East Lancs type I**

Following the success of the rebuilds of pre-war trolleybuses, a programme of rebuilding the first post-war vehicles was commenced in 1955 and this was continued almost continuously until 1963. The first rebuilds involved new East Lancashire Coachbuilders 72 seat bodies of a pleasing, modern appearance. Eighteen vehicles were initially dealt with, mostly from the DVH registered group, in three batches of six as follows:

553, 554, 555, 556, 557, 558
551, 552, 559, 560, 561, 563
562, 564, 565, 566, 570, 573

The last six had slightly shorter front dash panels. From 1960 onwards, many of these trolleybuses had their front and rear bumpers removed following overhaul or accident damage. In 1963, the bodies from withdrawn vehicles 556,557,561 and 563 were overhauled and transferred onto the chassis of 586, 587, 591 and 592. (see photograph 96). The view here shows 562 in its original rebuilt form. It is at the alighting stop for the Bradford Road / Birkby routes at the north end of John William Street. Withdrawals of this type started in 1962, although 553, 554 and 555, together with the quartet with second-hand bodies, lasted until July 1965. (S.Lockwood coll.)

114. **Karrier/Sunbeam MS2 rebuilds - Roe**

Further contracts for the rebuilding of the 1947-1949 series of vehicles were awarded to Roe who built fifteen bodies in three batches of five in 1958 and 1959. The trolleybuses involved were:

550, 567, 568, 569, 571
572, 574, 575, 576, 577
578, 579, 580, 581, 589

These bodies introduced glass fibre domes and metal, instead of wood, interior fittings. They were visually similar to the twenty bodies supplied to Rotherham in 1956/57 to rebuild their single deck trolleybuses. The last group of five had a lower deck emergency window and did not have bumpers. A few of the others had these features removed during their life. The photograph shows 575 immediately before delivery. These vehicles were withdrawn between 1963 and 1965. (R. Marshall coll.)

115. **Karrier / Sunbeam MS2 rebuilds - East Lancs type II**

The final group of trolleybuses to be rebuilt (apart from the second hand bodies described under photograph 113) were eight trolleybuses given East Lancashire bodies in 1961 / 2. These vehicles were 543,545,546,548 in 1961 and 582,583,584 and 585 in 1962. 585, shown here, carried the last trolleybus body built for a three axle chassis for British use. The design followed closely the East Lancashire bodies built on new chassis in 1959 (see photograph 118). The first withdrawal came in 1964 when 545 suffered severe rear end damage and the remainder lasted until 1967 with 548 being the very last in service. The handsome lines of these bodies are evident in this view at Lockwood terminus. Note that the front dash panel is divided and joined by a central metal strip. This was probably a result of accident repairs.
(J.S.King)

116. **593 - 599 FCX 293 - 299**
600 - 606 FCX 800 - 806

These vehicles had Sunbeam MS2 chassis with Roe 70 seat bodies, which were a longer version of those supplied to the rebuilt pre-war Karrier E6 vehicles described earlier. They were delivered between 1950 and 1952 and the first one, 593, was exhibited on the Roe stand at the Commercial Motor Show in London in 1950. Because of this it was supplied with gold lining, red bumpers instead of black and had non-standard seat trim. All the others were supplied in conventional livery as shown here. These vehicles subsequently lost their bumpers and Sunbeam badges as well as the dipped mudguards over the rear wheels with which most of this type were fitted. Withdrawals commenced at the end of 1964 with 594 but most remained in service until July 1966. (J.Copland)

→

117. **607 - 618 GVH 807 - 818**
619 - 630 KVH 219 - 229, 930

The next vehicles represented a change from the Karrier / Sunbeam types of almost all previous Huddersfield trolleys. These had BUT 9641T chassis with East Lancashire 72 seat bodies almost identical to the bodies being supplied for rebuilt vehicles. There were two batches, numbers 607 to 618 entering service in 1953 and the remainder in 1956. The later KVH registered ones had slightly shorter front dash panels. These vehicles were arguably the most impressive looking trolleybuses in the fleet and were very highly regarded. All except 609 lost their bumpers from 1959 onwards and withdrawals commenced in 1966. Six (615, 616, 617, 618, 625 and 626) were stored out of use between November 1961 and October 1962 together with two MS2s (605 and 606). Most of the KVH registered batch lasted until the end of the system with numbers 623 and 629 performing the final runs. The first of the KVH registered batch, 619, is seen in original condition. This vehicle still exists in working order at Sandtoft Transport Centre. (R.F.Mack)

(below)
118. **631 - 640** **PVH 931 - 940**
These were the final new trolleybuses bought by Huddersfield and they entered service in late 1959. They had Sunbeam S7 chassis and East Lancashire 72 seat bodies. Although modern in appearance, they continued the conservative Huddersfield specification of being only 7 feet 6 inches wide and having three axles and were thus the last three-axle trolleybus chassis built for British service. In contrast, nearby Bradford was, at the same time, having built by the same coachbuilder, trolleybus bodies with front entrance, air powered doors, and heaters, luxuries that no Huddersfield trolleybus passenger ever enjoyed. Not as well liked or as reliable as the BUT trolleys, some of these Sunbeams saw prolonged periods out of service awaiting spares and they had a disturbing transmission groan when operating at higher speeds. Nevertheless the S7s ran until the last year of the system apart from 634 which was prematurely retired - (see photograph 56). Nos 638 and 640 operated on the final day. This photograph shows the final vehicle, 640, with the distinctive towing hatch on the front dash that was unique to these vehicles, at Lockwood Bar negotiating the turn into Bridge Street. (S.Ledgard)

FINALE

119. BUT 623 was selected to be the decorated 'last' trolleybus which would carry the mayor and civic party on the final run to Waterloo and Outlane on Saturday afternoon, 13th July 1968. The vehicle was lavishly decorated with suitable lettering and white painted trolley booms, and was illuminated as shown. It entered service in this form on Monday 8th July and worked in normal all-day service up to Friday 12th July. At night it was particularly attractive, with the illuminations winking off then on whenever 623 passed over a dead section in the overhead. The end of the trolleys was also commemorated by the issue of souvenir tickets on all trolleys during the last week. A commemorative brochure was also issued. On the last day, 623 loaded the civic party for the last run in St George's Square and is seen here having turned from Railway Street into Westgate to follow 629. The crowds here and along all the route were quite considerable reflecting the genuine affection which Huddersfield people had for their trolleys. (P.Lockwood)

120. The only two trolleys turned out for service on the last day were 640 on route 71 and 629 on route 73. All the other workings were allocated to new Fleetline diesel buses. 638 was stationed in St George's Square as a spare vehicle and was called upon to take over at midday when 640 failed in Westgate and was towed away, its working life over. 629, which would work the last public trolleybus journey, ran with a full standing load well before the last round trip. This commenced at 2.31pm in Westgate, running to Waterloo then through to Outlane and finishing back at Westgate. For this trip, additional trolleys were brought out to run in front of 629, these being 626, 627 and 638 with 623 following as the last Civic trolleybus. After the last journey was over, 629 was wisely allowed to run back in service to Longroyd Bridge Depot. Because 623 was towed away from St George's Square directly to Great Northern Street Works, 629 became Huddersfield's last trolleybus to carry passengers. It can be seen heeling over with its capacity load as it turns from St George's Square into John William Street to travel through the town centre en route to Longroyd Bridge for the last time. (S.Ledgard)

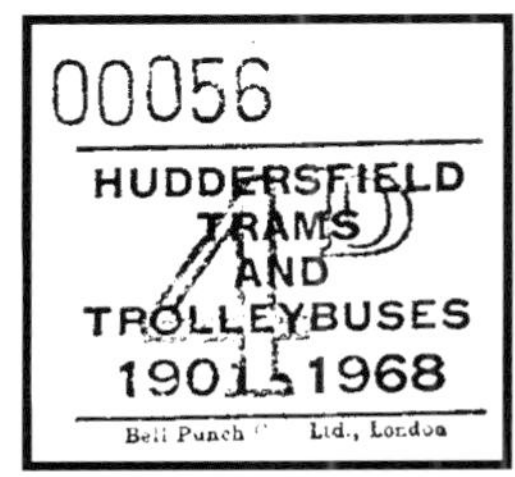

LAST WEEK OF
TROLLEYBUS
OPERATION
7th-13th JULY
1968
Issued subject to
Regulations

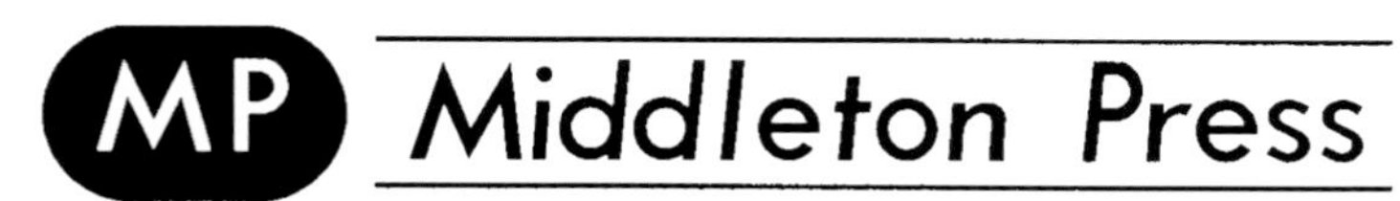

Easebourne Lane, Midhurst, W Sussex. GU29 9AZ Tel: 01730 813169 Fax: 01730 812601

If books are not available from your local transport stockist, order direct with cheque, Visa or Mastercard, post free UK.

BRANCH LINES
Branch Line to Allhallows
Branch Line to Alton
Branch Lines around Ascot
Branch Line to Ashburton
Branch Lines around Bodmin
Branch Line to Bude
Branch Lines around Canterbury
Branch Lines around Chard & Yeovil
Branch Line to Cheddar
Branch Lines around Cromer
Branch Lines to East Grinstead
Branch Lines of East London
Branch Lines to Effingham Junction
Branch Lines around Exmouth
Branch Lines to Falmouth, Helston & St. Ives
Branch Line to Fairford
Branch Lines around Gosport
Branch Line to Hayling
Branch Lines to Henley, Windsor & Marlow
Branch Line to Hawkhurst
Branch Lines around Huntingdon
Branch Line to Ilfracombe
Branch Line to Kingswear
Branch Line to Lambourn
Branch Lines to Launceston & Princetown
Branch Line to Looe
Branch Line to Lyme Regis
Branch Lines around Midhurst
Branch Line to Minehead
Branch Line to Moretonhampstead
Branch Lines to Newport
Branch Lines to Newquay
Branch Lines around North Woolwich
Branch Line to Padstow
Branch Lines around Plymouth
Branch Lines to Seaton and Sidmouth
Branch Lines around Sheerness
Branch Line to Shrewsbury
Branch Line to Swanage *updated*
Branch Line to Tenterden
Branch Lines around Tiverton
Branch Lines to Torrington
Branch Line to Upwell
Branch Lines of West London
Branch Lines around Weymouth
Branch Lines around Wimborne
Branch Lines around Wisbech

NARROW GAUGE
Branch Line to Lynton
Branch Lines around Portmadoc 1923-46
Branch Lines around Porthmadog 1954-94
Branch Line to Southwold
Douglas to Port Erin
Douglas to Peel
Kent Narrow Gauge
Northern France Narrow Gauge
Romneyrail
Southern France Narrow Gauge
Sussex Narrow Gauge
Two-Foot Gauge Survivors
Vivarais Narrow Gauge

SOUTH COAST RAILWAYS
Ashford to Dover
Bournemouth to Weymouth
Brighton to Worthing
Eastbourne to Hastings
Hastings to Ashford
Portsmouth to Southampton
Ryde to Ventnor
Southampton to Bournemouth

SOUTHERN MAIN LINES
Basingstoke to Salisbury
Bromley South to Rochester
Crawley to Littlehampton
Dartford to Sittingbourne
East Croydon to Three Bridges
Epsom to Horsham
Exeter to Barnstaple
Exeter to Tavistock
Faversham to Dover
London Bridge to East Croydon
Orpington to Tonbridge
Tonbridge to Hastings
Salisbury to Yeovil
Sittingbourne to Ramsgate
Swanley to Ashford
Tavistock to Plymouth
Three Bridges to Brighton
Victoria to Bromley South
Victoria to East Croydon
Waterloo to Windsor
Waterloo to Woking
Woking to Portsmouth
Woking to Southampton
Yeovil to Exeter

EASTERN MAIN LINES
Barking to Southend
Ely to Kings Lynn
Ely to Norwich
Fenchurch Street to Barking
Ipswich to Saxmundham
Liverpool Street to Ilford
Saxmundham to Yarmouth
Tilbury Loop

WESTERN MAIN LINES
Didcot to Swindon
Ealing to Slough
Exeter to Newton Abbot
Newton Abbot to Plymouth
Newbury to Westbury
Paddington to Ealing
Paddington to Princes Risborough
Plymouth to St. Austell
Princes Risborough to Banbury
Reading to Didcot
Slough to Newbury
St. Austell to Penzance
Taunton to Exeter
Westbury to Taunton

MIDLAND MAIN LINES
Euston to Harrow & Wealdstone
St. Pancras to St. Albans

COUNTRY RAILWAY ROUTES
Abergavenny to Merthyr
Andover to Southampton
Bath to Evercreech Junction
Bournemouth to Evercreech Junction
Burnham to Evercreech Junction
Cheltenham to Andover
Croydon to East Grinstead
Didcot to Winchester
East Kent Light Railway
Fareham to Salisbury
Guildford to Redhill
Reading to Basingstoke
Reading to Guildford
Redhill to Ashford
Salisbury to Westbury
Stratford upon Avon to Cheltenham
Strood to Paddock Wood
Taunton to Barnstaple
Wenford Bridge to Fowey
Westbury to Bath
Woking to Alton
Yeovil to Dorchester

GREAT RAILWAY ERAS
Ashford from Steam to Eurostar
Clapham Junction 50 years of change
Festiniog in the Fifties
Festiniog in the Sixties
Festiniog 50 years of enterprise
Isle of Wight Lines 50 years of change
Railways to Victory 1944-46
Return to Blaenau 1970-82
SECR Centenary album
Talyllyn 50 years of change
Yeovil 50 years of change

LONDON SUBURBAN RAILWAYS
Caterham and Tattenham Corner
Charing Cross to Dartford
Clapham Jn. to Beckenham Jn.
Crystal Palace (HL) & Catford Loop
East London Line
Finsbury Park to Alexandra Palace
Holbourn Viaduct to Lewisham
Kingston and Hounslow Loops
Lewisham to Dartford
Lines around Wimbledon
London Bridge to Addiscombe
Mitcham Junction Lines
North London Line
South London Line
West Croydon to Epsom
West London Line
Willesden Junction to Richmond
Wimbledon to Beckenham
Wimbledon to Epsom

STEAMING THROUGH
Steaming through Cornwall
Steaming through the Isle of Wight
Steaming through Kent
Steaming through West Hants
Steaming through West Sussex

TRAMWAY CLASSICS
Aldgate & Stepney Tramways
Barnet & Finchley Tramways
Bath Tramways
Brighton's Tramways
Bristol's Tramways
Burton & Ashby Tramways
Camberwell & W.Norwood Tramways
Clapham & Streatham Tramways
Croydon's Tramways
Dover's Tramways
East Ham & West Ham Tramways
Edgware and Willesden Tramways
Eltham & Woolwich Tramways
Embankment & Waterloo Tramways
Enfield & Wood Green Tramways
Exeter & Taunton Tramways
Greenwich & Dartford Tramways
Hammersmith & Hounslow Tramways
Hampstead & Highgate Tramways
Hastings Tramways
Holborn & Finsbury Tramways
Ilford & Barking Tramways
Kingston & Wimbledon Tramways
Lewisham & Catford Tramways
Liverpool Tramways 1. Eastern Routes
Liverpool Tramways 2. Southern Routes
Liverpool Tramways 3. Northern Routes
Maidstone & Chatham Tramways
Margate to Ramsgate
North Kent Tramways
Norwich Tramways
Reading Tramways
Seaton & Eastbourne Tramways
Shepherds Bush & Uxbridge Tramways
Southend-on-sea Tramways
Southwark & Deptford Tramways
Stamford Hill Tramways
Twickenham & Kingston Tramways
Victoria & Lambeth Tramways
Waltham Cross & Edmonton Tramways
Walthamstow & Leyton Tramways
Wandsworth & Battersea Tramways

TROLLEYBUS CLASSICS
Croydon Trolleybuses
Derby Trolleybuses
Hastings Trolleybuses
Huddersfield Trolleybuses
Maidstone Trolleybuses
Portsmouth Trolleybuses
Woolwich & Dartford Trolleybuses

WATERWAY ALBUMS
Kent and East Sussex Waterways
London to Portsmouth Waterway
West Sussex Waterways

MILITARY BOOKS
Battle over Portsmouth
Battle over Sussex 1940
Bombers over Sussex 1943-45
Bognor at War
Military Defence of West Sussex
Military Signals from the South Coast
Secret Sussex Resistance
Surrey Home Guard

OTHER RAILWAY BOOKS
Index to all Middleton Press stations
Industrial Railways of the South-East
South Eastern & Chatham Railways
London Chatham & Dover Railway
War on the Line (SR 1939-45)

BIOGRAPHY
Garraway Father & Son